THE NEW
POCKET GUIDE
Ingenious Blend of Chinese and Western Signs
SUZANNE WHITE

THE NEW ASTROLOGY
Your Pocket Guide

A Short Trip To The Land of The New Astrology

By Suzanne White

****

Published by:
Suzanne White

****

****

144 New Astrology Signs

THE ORIGINAL 600 PAGE NEW ASTROLOGY™
A FABULOUS BOOK
available from http://www.suzannewhite.com

Table of Contents

What Is the New Astrology?

The New Astrology compares Western signs to Chinese signs and comes up with 144 new signs. If you are a Sagittarius and were born in 1949, then you are a Sagittarius/Ox. Simple.

How Does the New Astrology Work?

The Chinese have divided time differently from us. We have 100-year centuries, the Chinese have periods of sixty years. We divide our centuries into ten decades. The Chinese divide their sixty-year spans into "dozencades" or twelve-year periods. At the end of each twelve-year period the Chinese cycle begins anew.

The twelve occidental months have celestial sign names: Aries, Taurus, Gemini, Cancer, Leo, Virgo, Libra, Scorpio, Sagittarius, Capricorn, Aquarius, Pisces. The twelve oriental years have animal sign names: Rat, Ox, Tiger, Cat, Dragon, Snake, Horse, Goat, Monkey, Rooster, Dog, Pig. In both cases the astrological sign name refers to the character of people born under its influence.

There are 144 New Astrology signs. Each is a combined East/West sign. Consult the calendar tables below. Take your regular, familiar astrological sign and match it with the animal sign of the year you were born. Now you have your NEW ASTROLOGY sign! Find your western sign in the bookmarks to the left and... YOU ARE THERE!

The Western Astrological Reference Chart

In a Western astrological year there are twelve signs. Each sign lasts for about one month. They are established in the following order:

DATES | SIGN

21 MARCH-19 APRIL | ARIES

20 APRIL-20 MAY | TAURUS

21 MAY621 JUNE | GEMINI

22 JUNE-22 JULY | CANCER

23 JULY-22 AUGUST | LEO

23 AUGUST-22 SEPTEMBER | VIRGO

23 SEPTEMBER-23 OCTOBER | LIBRA

24 OCTOBER-21 NOVEMBER | SCORPIO

22 NOVEMBER-21 DECEMBER | SAGITTARIUS

22 DECEMBER-19 JANUARY | CAPRICORN

20 JANUARY-18 FEBRUARY | AQUARIUS

19 FEBRUARY-20 MARCH | PISCES

The Chinese Astrology Reference Calendar

The Chinese New year starts later than ours. Hence the very long list of dates below:

Year | Sign | Year begins | Year ends

1900 | Rat | 01/31/1900 | 02/18/1901

1901 | Ox | 02/19/1901 | 02/07/1902

1902 | Tiger | 02/08/1902 | 01/28/1903

1903 | Cat | 01/29/1903 | 02/15/1904

1904 | Dragon | | 02/16/1904 | 02/03/1905

1905 | Snake | 02/04/1905 | 01/24/1906

1906 | Horse | 01/25/1906 | 02/12/1907

1907 | Goat | 02/13/1907 | 02/01/1908

1908 | Monkey | 02/02/1908 | 01/21/1909

1909 | Rooster | 01/22/1909 | 02/09/1910

1910 | Dog | 02/10/1910 | 01/29/1911

1911 | Pig | 01/30/1911 | 02/17/1912

1912 | Rat | 02/18/1912 | 02/05/1913

1913 | Ox | 02/06/1913 | 01/25/1914

1914 | Tiger | 01/26/1914 | 02/13/1915

1915 | Cat | 02/14/1915 | 02/02/1916

1916 | Dragon | 02/03/1916 | 01/22/1917

1917 | Snake | 01/23/1917 | 02/10/1918

1918 | Horse | 02/11/1918 | 01/31/1919

1919 | Goat | 02/01/1919 | 02/19/1920

1920 | Monkey | 02/20/1920 | 02/07/1921

1921 | Rooster | 02/08/1921 | 01/27/1922

1922 | Dog | 01/28/1922 | 02/15/1923

1923 | Pig | 02/16/1923 | 02/04/1924

1924 | Rat | 02/05/1924 | 01/23/1925

1925 | Ox | 01/24/1925 | 02/12/1926

1926 | Tiger | 02/13/1926 | 02/01/1927

1927 | Cat | 02/02/1927 | 01/22/1928

1928 | Dragon | 01/23/1928 | 02/09/1929

1929 | Snake | 02/10/1929 | 01/29/1930

1930 | Horse | 01/30/1930 | 02/16/1931

1931 | Goat | 02/17/1931 | 02/05/1932

1932 | Monkey | 02/06/1932 | 01/25/1933

1933 | Rooster | 01/26/1933 | 02/13/1934

1934 | Dog | 02/14/1934 | 02/03/1935

1935 | Pig | 02/04/1935 | 01/23/1936

1936 | Rat | 01/24/1936 | 02/10/1937

1937 | Ox | 02/11/1937 | 01/30/1938

1938 | Tiger | 01/31/1938 | 02/18/1939

1939 | Cat | 02/19/1939 | 02/07/1940

1940 | Dragon | 02/08/1940 | 01/26/1941

1941 | Snake | 01/27/1941 | 02/14/1942

1942 | Horse | 02/15/1942 | 02/04/1943

1943 | Goat | 02/05/1943 | 01/24/1944

1944 | Monkey | 01/25/1944 | 02/12/1945

1945 | Rooster | 02/13/1945 | 02/01/1946

1946 | Dog | 02/02/1946 | 01/21/1947

1947 | Pig | 01/22/1947 | 02/09/1948

1948 | Rat | 02/10/1948 | 01/28/1949

1949 | Ox | 01/29/1949 | 02/16/1950

1950 | Tiger | 02/17/1950 | 02/05/1951

1951 | Cat | 02/06/1951 | 01/26/1952

1952 | Dragon | 01/27/1952 | 02/13/1953

1953 | Snake | 02/14/1953 | 02/02/1954

1954 | Horse | 02/03/1954 | 01/23/1955

1955 | Goat | 01/24/1955 | 02/11/1956

1956 | Monkey | 02/12/1956 | 01/30/1957

1957 | Rooster | 01/31/1957 | 02/17/1958

1958 | Dog | 02/18/1958 | 02/07/1959

1959 | Pig | 02/08/1959 | 01/27/1960

1960 | Rat | 01/28/1960 | 02/14/1961

1961 | Ox | 02/15/1961 | 02/04/1962

1962 | Tiger | 02/05/1962 | 01/24/1963

1963 | Cat | 01/25/1963 | 02/12/1964

1964 | Dragon | 02/13/1964 | 02/01/1965

1965 | Snake | 02/02/1965 | 01/20/1966

1966 | Horse | 01/21/1966 | 02/08/1967

1967 | Goat | 02/09/1967 | 01/29/1968

1968 | Monkey | 01/30/1968 | 02/16/1969

1969 | Rooster | 02/17/1969 | 02/05/1970

1970 | Dog | 02/06/1970 | 01/26/1971

1971 | Pig | 01/27/1971 | 02/14/1972

1972 | Rat | 02/15/1972 | 02/02/1973

1973 | Ox | 02/03/1973 | 01/22/1974

1974 | Tiger | 01/23/1974 | 02/10/1975

1975 | Cat | 02/11/1975 | 01/30/1976

1976 | Dragon | 01/31/1976 | 02/17/1977

1977 | Snake | 02/18/1977 | 02/06/1978

1978 | Horse | 02/07/1978 | 01/27/1979

1979 | Goat | 01/28/1979 | 02/15/1980

1980 | Monkey | 02/16/1980 | 02/04/1981

1981 | Rooster | 02/05/1981 | 01/24/1982

1982 | Dog | 01/25/1982 | 02/12/1983

1983 | Pig | 02/13/1983 | 02/01/1984

1984 | Rat | 02/02/1984 | 02/19/1985

1985 | Ox | 02/20/1985 | 02/08/1986

1986 | Tiger | 02/09/1986 | 01/28/1987

1987 | Cat | 01/29/1987 | 02/16/1988

1988 | Dragon | 02/17/1988 | 02/05/1989

1989 | Snake | 02/06/1989 | 01/26/1990

1990 | Horse | 01/27/1990 | 02/14/1991

1991 | Goat | 02/15/1991 | 02/03/1992

1992 | Monkey | 02/04/1992 | 01/22/1993

1993 | Rooster | 01/23/1993 | 02/09/1994

1994 | Dog | 02/10/1994 | 01/30/1995

1995 | Pig | 01/31/1995 | 02/18/1996

1996 | Rat | 02/19/1996 | 02/06/1997

1997 | Ox | 02/07/1997 | 01/27/1998

1998 | Tiger | 01/28/1998 | 02/15/1999

1999 | Cat | 02/16/1999 | 02/04/2000

2000 | Dragon | 02/05/2000 | 01/23/2001

2001 | Snake | 01/24/2001 | 02/11/2002

2002 | Horse | 02/12/2002 | 01/31/2003

2003 | Goat | 02/01/2003 | 01/21/2004

2004 | Monkey | 01/22/2004 | 02/08/2005

2005 | Rooster | 02/09/2005 | 01/28/2006

2006 | Dog | 01/29/2006 | 02/17/2007

2007 | Pig | 02/18/2007 | 02/06/2008

2008 | Rat | 02/07/2008 | 01/25/2009

2009 | Ox | 01/26/2009 | 02/13/2010

2010 | Tiger | 02/14/2010 | 02/02/2011

2011 | Cat | 02/03/2011 | 01/22/2012

2012 | Dragon | 01/23/2012 | 02/09/2013

2013 | Snake | 02/10/2013 | 01/30/2014

2014 | Horse | 01/31/2014 | 02/18/2015

2015 | Goat | 02/19/2015 | 02/07/2016

2016 | Monkey | 02/08/2016 | 01/27/2017

2017 | Rooster | 01/28/2017 | 02/15/2018

2018 | Dog | 02/16/2018 | 02/04/2019

2019 | Pig | 02/05/2019 | 01/24/2020

ARIES

♈

ARIES/RAT - THE ARTFUL CHARMER

"Aries/Rat is the cleverest, wiliest and most loquacious of Aries alive. Rats are sociable. Aries are affable. Put the two together and you come up with personality plus. Blend the Rat's inimitable charisma with the dauntless self- assurance of Aries and you concoct yourself a winner. In bed? This go-getting person really delivers! He is no stranger to tender caresses and yet, the Aries/Rat fairly sizzles with raw passion..."

ARIES/OX - THE TIRELESS BULLDOZER

"The powerful Aries/Ox can wither a mountain in a halfhearted shrug. This is a mighty combination - doomed to achievement. The stalwart Aries character sallies forth into the world full of vigor and hope at a tender age. The Ox, solid and diligent, carries young Aries, head high, sword drawn, slowly but surely toward serious, demanding goals. Aries/Oxen are champions! Even in bed. These sure-footed creatures people understand sex at a visceral (gut) level..."

ARIES/TIGER- THE RIGHTEOUS DAREDEVIL

"The Tiger's taste for risk couples nicely here with the Aries' boyish courage. An Aries/Tiger is always someone nice to know, fun to be with and easy to like. Aries/Tigers are brimming with schemes and ideas. When they apply their multiple talents and energies, Aries/Tigers are unbeatably..."

ARIES/CAT-RABBIT – THE CAUTIOUS CARETAKER

"Caring is the Aries/Cat's specialty. Not only does this native care about everything solid and traditional and valuable, he also enjoys the capacity to care for those elements. This person is a generator of refinement, an accumulator of wisdom, a dispenser of metaphysical energy and a preserver of life's finer things. The Aries/Cat is quite simply a charmer... with claws and whiskers and occasional hissy fits guaranteed to spice up your sex life with..."

ARIES/DRAGON – THE ENTERPRISING PLAYBOY

"In the Aries/Dragon, we find a crackling combination of raw Aries energy and Dragon pluck and guile. It's an unbeatable concoction. Aries/Dragon burns to get ahead in life. Nothing can stop the brand of will and enterprise born into this subject. Solidly built and disgustingly healthy, this person exudes sexuality. So whenever..."

ARIES/SNAKE – THE BEWITCHING INNOVATOR

"This person is beautiful to look at and a pleasure to be with. Yet, inside, a Snake born Aries suffers pangs of contradiction. Does she tend the little fire or burn brightly with the big blazing one? Fiery Aries always wants to rush out and do and go and experience. The chilly Snake wants, on the other hand, to sit back and ponder, intuit and judge whilst warming her toes before her tiny fire. Whichever of her influences happens to be feeling stronger on any given day gets the upper hand. Where sex is concerned, you can just imagine! Beauty and the beast is an understatement..."

ARIES/HORSE – THE DAUNTLESS OPTIMIST

"There is something of the victorious athlete in all Aries/Horses. They are both fast on their feet and quick of wit. But they don't always carry through on their serve. Herein lies the first and most bothersome of Aries/Horse faults. Both Aries and Horse are pushy and active. Both signs are ego-oriented. Both Aries and Horse are guilty of willfulness. Couple them and you come up with a mighty character prone to demanding what he wants when he wants it, putting down his foot—after removing it from his mouth of course. The best part is however, that the Aries born Horse grows more kindly and sensitive with age. Nobody is ever bored in bed with an Aries/Horse. They approach sex with gusto and..."

ARIES/GOAT– THE NAÏVE GENIUS

"This highly creative character needs "social security" in order to survive. The nature of Aries/Goats is free-thinking, eccentric, and rebellious. But without an atmosphere of total safety and freedom from want in which to evolve without being forced to involve, this person will suffer. The talented Aries/Goat performs best with a tidy safety net. He or she wants structure, but prefers that structure come from others. Goats tend to be languorous and lovely in romantic situations except..."

ARIES/MONKEY– THE CRAFTY CHATTERBOX

"Talkers one and all, Aries/Monkeys are among the most forthright people around. If you ever get to know one and then leave her behind, I believe your most intense souvenir of her personality will be the things she said. Aries/Monkeys are famous for their directness in speech. They can talk your leg off. Always busy, directed and up to their slender necks in problem-solving, when they are not fixing the irreparable, Aries/Monkeys blaze new trails in the love department."

ARIES/ROOSTER – THE ARDENT GADABOUT

"The Aries/Rooster is a boiling teakettle of enthusiasm. Every single second of life for this character is full to overflowing with activity and gusto. Aries/Roosters would like to try everything at least once. And if these tests bring them pleasure or intense experience, they would like to try them again, please. This Aries is generous and outgoing, talented, versatile and curious to a fault. This person is like a spinning top. They twirl and whirl through life at breakneck speed until one day, they fall right over and stop. Then, they wait till someone or something starts them up again. If you fancy an Aries/Rooster, and feel up to being the starter, get ready for some creative sex when..."

ARIES/DOG – THE PETULANT SWEETHEART

"Aries and Dog both call up a spirit of naiveté. In the case of Aries there is the ever-present quality of soldierliness. Aries is a scout, a pioneer and as credulous as they come. He is so nice. Why shouldn't everybody else be nice too? The Dog is also quite nice. But he is also nervous and skeptical. Like Aries, the Dog wants to believe in the basic goodness of mankind. But he knows better. And that very knowledge can make him or her a shaking wreck. Kindly and giving of excellent advice, this person is also world famous for his or her ultra direct approach in the bedroom..."

ARIES/PIG - THE IMPASSIONED ANGEL

"Aries coupled with the Pig sign bespeaks an aura of comfort overlaid with rural enterprise. This is a sign whose subjects will not have an easy time, but the person's entourage, family, friends and colleagues will benefit from the most extraordinary friendship they may ever know. Aries/Pigs are kindness incarnate. They take bunches of squealing brats to movies and buy them all ice cream and let them drip it all over their clothes. The help out on every possible committee—including cleanup—and seem tireless about it all. But in more intimate circumstances, these people are sensuality incarnate. They go after sex..."

http://suzannewhite.com/astrology/newAstrology.html

Visit **http://suzannewhite.com** for Personal Chart Readings
Books, Horoscopes & Lifestyle Advice

TAURUS

♉

TAURUS/RAT - THE PROTECTIVE LEADER

"Taureans born in Rat years benefit from a happy accident. Rats are often hyper. The Taurus influence mitigates the Rat's piano-wire nervousness. And... to the lumbering Taurus personality, Rats adds spice, pizzazz and a hefty pinch of calculation. The Taurus/Rat is a combination of William Shakespeare and the Alexander the Great: tough, bright, with nerves of steel and natural superiority. In most life situations, their reputation for strength of purpose precedes them so (obviously) one is not surprised to discover this person's relentless, insistent ability to seduce and conquer."

TAURUS/OX - THE DELIBERATE DICTATOR

"It would seem at first glance that the combination of Taurus the Bull and his soul mate, the ominous Ox, might be so unwieldy and ponderous as to sink into extinction at the age of two months. The opposite, however, is true. Taureans born in Ox years do tend to be big, heavy characters. But they wield power handsomely. This blend of signs bestows weighty power on its subjects. They cannot help but rule and lead and supervise and take charge. Soften them up for sex? Not an easy task. This person is always up for a quick roll in the hay with a fair damsel or sexy bloke."

TAURUS/TIGER - THE RESOURCEFUL RULER

"The mind of the Taurean born Tiger is shipshape. Nothing that enters there gets out the other side without being carefully recorded. Tigers like to experience new things. Taureans want to hold on - to everything! This combination results in a redoubtably savvy character who, although he may seem slightly eccentric and just a smidgen too easygoing, is really keeping score while you're busy watching the grass grow. Taurus/Tiger not only keeps a weather eye. He was born with a raring-to-go sensuality. Be prepared for the ride of your life. This tawny beast likes to hang on tight to his prey, savor every limb and nuzzle every cranny."

TAURUS/CAT-RABBIT - THE AMBITIOUS HOMEBODY

"Security-oriented and vulnerable, this is a risky combination. Why? Because the Taurean born Cat requires safety and pledges and assurances and guarantees in all aspects of his life. He cannot function properly if the rent isn't paid and the kids don't all have new shoes. Taurus/Cat is not, by any stretch of the imagination, a bohemian. In fact, he is borderline bourgeois. Home and possessions are almost as important to this creature as sex. But still waters run deep. The seemingly reserved Taurus born in a Cat year is a veritable fund of silent surprises. Don't be surprised when he or she invites you to engage in some startlingly unusual sexual practices."

TAURUS/DRAGON – THE SILENT SHOWOFF

"Might and bite come together here, giving us a powerhouse of brutal energy and excessive adroitness. Nobody will ever tell you that they "just couldn't care less" about a Taurus/Dragon. People either adore Taurus Dragons or they detest them! On the one hand, this native exudes down-to the-ground good sense, but on the other he is tempestuously foolish and selfishly attention-getting. Taurus and Dragon form an unforgettable couple - a peripatetic love bug whose desires may suddenly shift from stuffy missionary to raunchy and rambunctious in what seems like a quest for pleasure at any cost. The sensuality quotient is exceedingly high in this fiery creature. Many sizzling sexual memories will be forged during lovemaking sessions with partners who dare to go all the way with a Taurus."

TAURUS/SNAKE – THE SLITHERING STOIC

"This is the most natural of Snakes. Snake people often display cosmic leanings and cleave to the other worldly. Taurus grounds them. This Snake will be intuitive (as usual), yet wonderfully discreet. The Taurus part of the character will lend earthiness. This wildly attractive creature causes havoc among members of the opposite (or same for that matter) sex. People cannot control their desire to be controlled by this marvelously sensual type whose alluring bedside manner is almost as dangerous in as it is out of bed. The steamy sexual reputation of this cool, yet earthy creature is legendary. When a Taurean born Snake wraps itself around a sex partner, the victim has absolutely no chance of (nor any desire for) escape."

TAURUS/HORSE – THE TALENTED TYRANT

"Greedy for dominion over others, the Taurus/Horse wants to play the beau role in all of life's dramas. The Horse is a prancer and even when housed in the mind and body of the earthbound Taurus, that old pony will kick up his heels, show who's boss and even occasionally throw his rider—just to keep the record straight. How can this egomaniacal demi-genius stop preening long enough to love anyone? Well, the fact is that Love can be the undoing of this Horse. Thunderous love-at-first-sight is not uncommon and often leads this person to ruination. You see, this Horse appears reserved, almost intellectual. But between the sheets, like all good steeds, this Horse is a private dynamo."

TAURUS/GOAT – THE VOLATILE DREAMER

"This person is, by turns, a taciturn pixie, an industrious nitwit and a brilliant dreamer. Great genius often visits people born Taurus/Goat. And, if properly handled, this inner spark or enormous creative ability can take them far in both worldly and personal development. But without optimum growing conditions, this subject will spend his or her life seeming to putter about, half-finishing projects and only partially realizing dreams. Despite their somewhat delicate natures, these odd people hold claim to some of the most dramatic sexual exploits known to man (and woman). How to explain it? They are both tender and savage in bed."

TAURUS/MONKEY – THE UNSINKABLE WHIZ KID

"Here is one Monkey whose ruse and trickery are satisfied to remain in the wings for a lifetime. This is a fortuitous combination of signs. Equilibrium sticks out all over this steady, but wily creature. The Taurus/Monkey sets himself apart by dealing with trauma better than most. Beset by loss or struck down by tragedy, this creature remains buoyant through it all. This Monkey is particularly attractive to his sexual opposites. It's the eternal child side that we all find so irresistible."

TAURUS/ROOSTER – THE VALIANT CRUSADER

"Great wisdom and authority characterize the Taurean born in Rooster years. This person is self-possessed in the extreme. Taurus endows him with unshakable determination. Rooster lends enthusiasm and blind faith. From an early age, the Taurus/Rooster exhibits a tendency to dominate. Taurus/Roosters are, however, not usually political leaders. Taurus/Rooster is quite simply, fearlessly and naturally prominent. In the bedroom however, the Taurus/Rooster is a more laid back. He's a no-holds-barred compassionate lover."

TAURUS/DOG – THE DISQUIET MASTER

"Here is a dutiful combination gifted for performances of all kinds and cursed by a surfeit of uneasiness, which easily translates into dissatisfaction. Let me explain. Taureans born in Dog years tend to complain a lot. They find fault with much of what life offers, As for what life doesn't offer—they feel it should. Taurus/Dogs have an overdeveloped sense of injustice. They cannot understand why it seems as if the cards are always stacked against them. Why are others so lucky? Why do things seem to just fall into their laps? Why don't wonderful lucky things happen to me? Grumbles the dissatisfied Taurus/Dog. But this person doesn't stay unsatisfied for long. He or she is sexy beyond sexy.

TAURUS/PIG – THE RUSTIC SOPHISTICATE

"You are likely to find one of these subjects among the "beautiful people." Taureans born in Pig years, albeit rather rustic in certain ways, are attracted to the upper levels of society. Material wealth will serve to embellish the opulent life of the Taurean/Pig. He enjoys both riches and position and, frankly. Never accepts less than what he feels is his absolute due (lots). This person is also quite bossy. He needs to have his own way. He will cooperate. But only if he gets to be the "Mommy." Not so in Bed. The Taurus born Pig surrenders willingly in satin sheets. Bring him or her bonbons and finest chocolates too much. Pour champagne on his tootsies."

GEMINI

♊

GEMINI/RAT – THE PERPETUAL COMMUNICATOR

"A shooting star of infinite genius and practically no end of tales to tell, your average Gemini/Rat flits amiably around the room at any and all gatherings, charming and bright, delighted and delightful. Catch me if you can. And the fact is you can. But you must first discover Gemini/Rat's secret password. The key to the Gemini/Rat's most guarded intimacy is "I." This character observes the world through an almost impenetrable haze of ego. Geminis born in Rat years blend the flittery-fluttery Gemini spirit with the Rat's excessive nervousness. Both signs thrive on motion. Just think of it! A butterfly with a jet engine inside, moving all the time, busy at applying talents he doesn't even know he has. The Gemini/Rat is a generous person. Especially in intimate sexual situations."

GEMINI/OX –THE PROFLIGATE TRADITIONALIST

"Ox is a boon to the Gemini's blithe spirit. This is an almost settling down Gemini - a family sort of Gemini with eyes for the good life. A Gemini born Ox will always go forward, albeit more deliberately and ponderously than other Geminis, toward goals big and small. This Gemini is a thinker, yes. But he's not guilty of leaping from thought number one to idea number thirty-three and back to thought number one in two seconds flat. Concentration is more than possible and great work may even be accomplished. Under the quilt, this armchair lothario will work characteristically harder than most to do the job "right". "

GEMINI/TIGER – THE BENEVOLENT SPEED DEMON

"What this impetuous person needs most is good brakes. When you combine hotheadedness with mercurial tendencies, you get some very smart dynamite. The pep and seductiveness of this character has a sort of generous pussycat congeniality to top it off. It's pretty delectable to behold. But it's very difficult to hang on to. As Gemini never stops darting from pillar to post, philosophy to news flash, project to love affair, the character is already injected with a large dose of blast-off fuel. To add to the instability, along lopes our old friend the tawny Tiger, whose basic idea of himself is that he is extraordinary, ought to be chosen king of the jungle right now if not sooner and would you please move over so he can sit down on that throne? In the bedroom? Well, just imagine the rending of garments and gnashing of teeth which accompany this sexy character's lovemaking style."

GEMINI/CAT-RABBIT – THE PRUDENT REBEL

"Cat and Gemini make strange bedfellows. The discreet, prudent, careful Cat character infused with Gemini's mercurial pizzazz gives me pause to ponder how in the world such a person might achieve self-knowledge and control. I mean, look at the problem. Geminis are all sizzle and snap. Cats, on the other hand, tend to gentility, caution, comfort. To me it seems the busy Gemini rushing about tilting at a huge variety of windmills must, when born in Cat years, from time to time feel himself suddenly leapt upon—surprise!—by his feline-nature mate whose padded feet dart out sharp claws to remind the Gemini, "Take it easy. Go slow. Back off. Sit still. Don't grab.

Hang back. Beware." Mild schizophrenia. But charming in the extreme and a veritable surprise package in the bedroom. This person's subtle sexuality shows up in scores of imaginative ways."

GEMINI/DRAGON – THE SHIMMERING WIZARD

"The active, aerated Gemini mind couples brilliantly with our friend the dashing Dragon. Gemini/Dragons are exciting and bewitching. They have élan to burn and charm galore. Gemini/Dragons personify panache. But don't count on them to perform any mental gymnastic that requires more than ten minutes' concentration. The hot fire of novelty burns brightly and excites this subject to create great dreams and formulate giant plans. But the Gemini/Dragon is easily bored. He sincerely wants the living room to be painted a beautiful creamy white by the time the guests arrive this weekend. But he cannot stop watching the tennis on TV long enough to go buy the paint. Sexuality incarnate, this love demon can never get enough. The Gemini born Dragon wants more and knows how to go after it by devious and delightful means."

GEMINI/SNAKE - THE RADIANT PHILOSOPHER

"A paradoxical character is the Gemini/Snake. If he can get a good grip on the specialness that is his natural endowment from birth, this person is qualified for true greatness. The Gemini/Snake is a deep thinker. Imagine the lucky combination of reflection, performance and intuition! The marriage of the two signs is fortuitous indeed But this heady mixture of influences is a veritable minefield of pitfalls as well. People born in Gemini/Snake are sitting ducks for both Byzantine self-delusion and rank laziness. Invertebrate inertia, fueled by an oddly sunny irony, creates here a character of charisma unbound. Big brains, beauty and plenty of sexual pizzazz often join forces to skyrocket this person to overnight success and even stardom. This magnetic soul's legendary sexual skills are never idle. The luscious Gemini/Snake gives value for investment in the bedroom."

GEMINI/HORSE – THE STRUTTING ALTRUIST

The Horse's stylish bearing measured against the Gemini mutability gives us a multitalented person whose own worst enemy is himself. There's a nagging little gremlin wringing his hands inside the head of this goodhearted character who says, "I don't have to take this garbage! I don't have to put up with this nonsense! I want my freedom. I want my soul back." Of course we all know that our soul is never our own. But the Gemini/Horse works very hard to disprove that. He wants to be different, unusual, better than everybody else, cleverer, sexier, better dressed, and most of all, coolest. Yes, the Gemini/Horse wants desperately to be considered cool, one of the gang, a terrific fellow. Gemini/Horses can stick to their work. Normally, they choose a career that interests them and go ahead with that forever. They are often talented in music or graphic arts and are usually, in some very important way, involved in theatrical endeavors. Gemini/Horses are circus horses. Instead of walking, they prance. Their lovability quotient is high, but their ability to return love is often compromised. However, once they find themselves in sizzling sexual situations, like all Horses, they perform handsomely."

GEMINI/GOAT – THE ELEGANT COQUETTE

The Gemini/Goat is a firefly who flits about in others' lives out of sheer caprice; a tired pessimist who denigrates and disagrees with the world at large; or perhaps he's the eternally disappointed critic whose longing for perfection (in others, of course) leads him to drop acerbic comments as though they were rose petals. The Gemini/Goat is a bit of a lot of different things. You won't find many Goats running around loose. Goats need other people. All Goats require both company and guiding forces. Gemini is the mercurial sign: quick, volatile, fickle. So put these together. Dependency and fickleness. Like a smiling, chubby baby who's looking around for a change from his dull parents and leaps into the arms of almost anybody who passes his stroller in the street. Obviously, this versatile person makes a fabulous – if temporary – lover. When they find themselves in bed with one, they may well be thinking of the next or the last great lovemaking session. Butterflies in bed, they can think up the most ingenious sex games."

GEMINI/MONKEY -THE INSUBORDINATE SHOWMAN

"Monkeys and Geminis resemble each other. When I consider the energy level of this New Astrology sign, it's as though someone took twelve Monkeys, piled them on top of a dozen sets of twins, tailed a couple of Rolls-Royce jet engines and then let 'er rip. These people never cease moving. In fact, I wonder if Gemini/Monkeys ever sleep. Gemini/Monkeys love to talk. They need to perform, and even, I am afraid, to show off. For this reason, Gemini/Monkeys enjoy entertaining and watching others have a good time. They plan giant festivals and feasts complete with hand-opened oysters and lobsters flown in from the farthest reaches of the earth. They hold magical power over others and are adored by their lovers and spouses. Sex? Well, yes. Gemini/Monkeys are sexy. But the sex here is cloudy, murky – perhaps more intriguing than with some ordinary signs."

GEMINI/ROOSTER - THE COURTLY CAVALIER

"The performing Gemini is herein blessed with a complement of the Rooster persuasion. Performance meets grit. Rooster loves to swagger and swashbuckle, wears finery with aplomb and carries it all off as though he'd been born in a backstage wardrobe trunk. Gemini/Roosters, as actors or teachers or doctors or show business personalities, have it all over their competition. Talent? Yes. These people do have a certain amount of interpretive skill. But their strongest card is resilience. This Gemini/Rooster is a walking trampoline. Nothing, not illness, not rejection, not sorrow or self-pity, can keep this good person down. The sex lives of attractive Gemini/Roosters are epic. Everybody wants to sleep with this gorgeous creature. The men are often born Don Juans and the women willing sexual partners. The kind of sex this character gets up to is certainly not ordinary."

GEMINI/DOG – THE RESOURCEFUL CLOWN

"This is the one Dog subject who escapes the knitted brow and ready bark of many Dog characters. The Gemini's sociability lends exactly the right amount of levity to the disquiet Dog's nature. The Gemini/Dog is a bouncy person with many talents and aptitudes who needs, above everything, to adhere faithfully to the rules. Otherwise, if a Gemini/Dog swerves off course, tests authority and tries to get by with less than true hard work and grit, or tries to cheat his way to success, disaster will ensue. Altruism is the Dog's special quarter. People born in Dog years are forever taking up causes and joining crusades for the sake of their fellow human beings. Dogs are good people. The addition here of lighthearted Gemini, with his talent for the verbal and ability to amuse and even show off, to the steady, hardworking and worried Dog person's life is a mixed godsend. Either this Dog will spend too much of himself on the woes of the world and of others, or if, alas, he has allowed the Gemini superficiality to run away with him, he may not give a pig's whistle about others. His or her sexual prowess is legendary. This person is a seduction machine par excellence. Don't expect the humdrum missionary approach."

GEMINI/PIG – THE INDUSTRIOUS CONNOISSEUR

"The Gemini born in a Pig year boasts the double blessing of versatility and scrupulousness. Pigs, as we already know, seek riches and know how to cultivate the best in life. But they can sometimes be a bit sluggish too, and quite stubborn in their own peculiar way. The mercurial Gemini adds levity to the good Pig's dowdy nature, buoys up his occasional spells of dark wrath and lends action to this character's existence. You will note that a Gemini/Pig can seem as busy as an Eskimo trying to save his house in a heat wave. He's rushing hither and thither, darting everywhere at once. At another time, you'll find this character sprawled on a silken divan chomping bonbons of finest Swiss chocolate, positively languishing in affluent sloth. Gemini is double-faced and despite the solidity that Pig brings to this person, he cannot escape the need to feel free to dash off in at least two directions on any subject or in any situation. This voluptuous person attracts money. And he also attracts the opposite (or same) sex."

http://suzannewhite.com/astrology/newAstrology.html

CANCER

♋

CANCER/RAT – THE RECLUSIVE CHATTERBOX

"Because he is born a Rat, the Cancer/Rat naturally lives by his wits. But as he is also a moon child and hence tends to drown in his own emotions this person's behavior wavers. The Cancer/Rat, we say, is a "private" person. He likes to crawl into his cubbyhole in the tower where he studies life and writes about interior subjects. But just when you think the Cancer/Rat has hidden away for good, will only venture out for the odd crust of bread and seems to be surviving on coffee and water up there in that tomblike turret, an invitation arrives at your door requesting the honor of your company at a huge reception complete with great groaning boards of food and gaiety and sociability to boot. Who is your host or hostess but your favorite recluse, the Cancer/Rat. Falling in love with a Cancer born Rat is like becoming an overnight prince or princess. You will be competently courted, lavishly seduced and when you finally fall into this creature's capable arms, you will swoon...".

CANCER/OX – THE RELENTLESS CREATIVE

"It is no coincidence that many, many famous and respected artists of all sorts were born under the twin signs of Cancer and Ox. Here is the personification of determination. The profound sensitivity of Cancer coupled with the Ox's down-to-earth strength of purpose creates in this creature an emotional forcefulness unparalleled anywhere else in the new zodiac. This person always tries harder. The Ox side of this subject's character endows him or her with formidable powers of tenacity and innovation. Cancer lends even more creativity and adds a hefty dose of feeling to the cocktail. These folks go after what they want with acute single-mindedness. For a Cancer/Ox a task is a chore is a rule is a religion! What must be accomplished must be, and there are no two ways about it, no shortcuts, and no tricky escape routes. This often famous person's sex life is of the utmost importance to them. Yet, he or she maintains a discreet distance from prying press and flashing paparazzi. Intimacy, to this busily creative person, is just that. Intimate. Private. Secret and oh-so sensuous."

CANCER/TIGER – THE DOLEFUL DYNAMO

"There is a lot of true sentiment running around wild here. The worst enemy of this restless, moody character is loss of confidence. Without some serious bolstering, he or she may well surrender to a dissolute, rudderless existence. Tigers need to learn moderation and control their excessiveness. Tigers should seek good counsel, advice, wisdom and common sense. Cancer is, for the most part, a sensible sign. But then, Cancers are darkly emotional and can drown in a single fit of melancholy. The challenge for this sexy person is to find true love. Someone to rely on, to care deeply about and be cared for in return. If this goal is met, Cancer/Tigers thrive and their lovers never regret a single steamy intimate encounter as this subject is a sexual dynamo."

CANCER/CAT-RABBIT – THE HOMESPUN POWERHOUSE

"A startling combination of home-loving and home-loving, if the Cancer/Cat didn't have to go out to make a living, he indeed might opt to never leave the comfort of his perfectly decorated, carefully appointed and cozily efficient house. To a Cancer born a Cat, the center of his universe is his hearth. If he has any enemies, they will only be able to really wound the Cancer/Cat where it hurts if they attack his epicenter—the home. This person is not a recluse. On the contrary. Once he gets to know you, Cancer/Cat is a veritable bundle of amiability and chitchat. He lights up when he sees you and talk about your favorite subjects -just to please you. Often, this person talks of things to come, dreams and future plans of castles (always castles or manor houses or mansions) in Spain or Normandy or in the lush green dank of Ireland. Faithful in relationships, the Cancer born Cat excels at love with a capital L."

CANCER/DRAGON – THE SENTIMENTAL LUMINARY

"Great emotional vitality is the foundation of this astonishing character's personality. The Cancer/Dragon is born with all of Cancer's profound ability to feel life in every aspect. This subject is also endowed with Dragonish pluck. So we have here a forceful and dauntlessly enthusiastic character. Cancer's eternal black moods will be lightened by the Dragon's phoenix-like ability to rise from the ashes of his own immolation by his natural pep and vigor. Dragon's unwieldy braggadocio will be tempered by Cancer's good sense and dignity. Cancer/Dragon's got just a soupçon of a twinkle in a very sensual glance. Bedroom eyes with a skylight. Cancer wants to keep this subject home. Dragon longs to race out and beat the world at any game in town. Close contact with this dynamic soulful person is always satisfying. Tender? This person invented snuggles. The sex with this charmer is not to be misses."

CANCER/SNAKE - THE LAVISH LOVEBIRD

"As Cancers go, the Snake type is more independent of ponderous emotional fetters than his kin. He's familial to be sure, and even clinging—after all, he is both Snake and Cancer! But the Cancer born a Snake, unlike certain other Cancers we all know, recognizes his own weaknesses, comprehends his black moods and, because of his cool-headed sagacity, usually manages to slither out of the lunatic doldrums for which Cancers can be so famous. As Snakes go, the Cancer/Snake will be less cold-blooded than other serpents. Cancer's brooding soulfulness and profound affectivity lend the Snake a blanket, caress his cold exterior and warm the heart into something close to affability. In the Cancerian Snake, the tendency to want the leading role in all of life's movies is tempered by common sense and natural reserve. Needless to add that the sexual side of this highly sensitive (and attractive) person's life is of paramount importance. Get one of these into bed and then hang on for dear life."

CANCER/HORSE – THE MELANCHOLY WORKAHOLIC

"The Horse, you may recall, is able to give himself up to a romantic passion and chuck everything—including his self-respect—for the sake of love. Cancer/Horses are, with their Scorpio counterparts, about the most self sacrificing. Love and its vicissitudes, the preservation of a home and kids and pets and insurance policies and telephone bills, can all be capable taken in hand by the Cancer/Horse. When questioned as to why he continues to struggle so hard and so seemingly alone without compassion or cooperation, the Cancer/Horse merely smiles. "It's for Janet. I love her." Or "Its because of the children, my home, my family." Cancer born Horses make love the way they work. With zeal, technique and devotion to duty. If you ever get into bed with one of these passionate people, you won't want to get out."

CANCER/GOAT – THE SENSITIVE PROVIDER

"Cancer/Goat people bruise easily. They want to be solid citizens and go about their work taking care to see that things are in order and hoping that in the bargain everybody will be happy. They sincerely want everybody to have a good time, be honest and fair and hail-fellow-well-met. But the Cancer/Goat is too naively earnest. He should know better, he's been through some terrible disappointments in his time, but the Cancerian Goat persists in believing in Santa Claus and trusting in the basic goodness of mankind. Sex with this adorable lover is charged with affection. Caresses count for more than just foreplay when this person enters the bedroom."

CANCER/MONKEY – THE EMOTIONAL PLANNER

"This person is forever awake to new concepts and possible avenues. He's always on his toes. Even in the middle of the night, this variety of Cancer is raring to find out who makes the kinds of candles that exactly replicate church candles from Poland in the eighteenth century. Like all Monkeys, the Cancer/Monkey is a problem-solver. He can not only see a situation for what it is—as he is coldly objective when necessary—but he can see through cloudy dilemmas and for that reason come quickly to the end of them. The Cancer/Monkey lets very little grass grow under his feet. –especially when it come to love. Cancers born in Monkey years incessantly seek love wherever they can find it."

CANCER/ ROOSTER – THE CAUSTIC POLLYANNA

"Don't look to this warmhearted person for forgiveness. There is lots of deep Cancerian tenderness here. But there is also a great chunk of Rooster abrasiveness. This subject is secretly ambitious and, despite his jolly—even rotund— appearance, carries vengeance to its drastic conclusion every time. You may find him or her open and even charming at first. But try living next door to one of these folks. It can be a trial by fire. The outgoing side of this person's nature wants to be of assistance to others. He or she will show newcomers the ropes and volunteer to hand out programs at church on Sunday. But hold on. The Cancerian Rooster also boasts an irritable, cranky side. It's as though all the upfront heartiness had a dark and sinister lining. A veritable storehouse of sexuality lurks beneath the serious appearance of this subject whose epic sexploits may shock."

CANCER/DOG – THE FRETFUL MORALIST

"Omnipresent in the native of this sign is "feeling." Emotions run both deep and high in this sensitive—even touchy—character. Cancer/Dogs seem to carry a blinking sensor-beam radar system on their very skins. Everything affects them and affects them profoundly. A word, a glance or—God forbid—a harsh remark can dissolve these susceptible souls into a heap of nervous prostration. However uneasy they may be, Cancer/Dogs are oddly adventurous. In one way, they need protection from the big bad world and its vicissitudes. In another, they alleviate their fear by jumping on it with all four feet and wringing its neck. In love, the Cancer born Dog provides his or her mate with unflagging support, admiration and applause. In bed, these people are daring. They make love as though their lives depended on a positive outcome."

CANCER/PIG – THE OPENHANDED AUTOCRAT

The self-starter of all time, this person could live on a desert island, rise at dawn, say his prayers, prepare his tea, wash up, go to the rock that serves as the office, slave for fourteen straight hours, come back to his grass shack, prepare himself a huge feast, eat it, say his prayers, lie down under the palm tree and start again the next morning. Integrity is a word invented to describe Cancer/Pigs. They are whole, complete unto themselves, and require little other than fawning admiration, unflinching affection and obedient devotion from others. That's an exaggeration. Cancer/Pigs are utterly generous and charitable in the extreme. But they do like things their way and generally one way or the other see to it that the wheels turn in the direction they dictate. As far as love is concerned, they demand unflinching fidelity and are willing to return the favor – in spades! Sex is an everyday affair for this lusty creature whose ferocious sexual habits would make the Marquis de Sade blush blue."

LEO

♌

LEO/RAT – THE ANXIOUS DEBONAIR

The cinematic image that comes to mind when I ponder the combination of Leo and Rat is of Gene Kelly, umbrella in hand, dancing through teeming rain and singin' his heart out. Leo/Rats have it all over everybody for conjuring sunshine. They can make a party out of a thunderstorm more lavishly and efficiently than you can imagine possible. Leo/Rats' attributes are many, their faults serious but few. Enterprise is their strong suit. In bed as well as in the world outside, this person will undertake to manage things. He or she is a take-charge lover whose technique between the sheets is notable by it sizzling passion and direct approach."

LEO/OX – THE ARROGANT VICTOR

"Leadership and dominion combine here to create an unforgettably forceful personality type. The tone of rapport with Leo/Oxen never feels quite intimate or cozy enough. One wonders if there is really a heart beating inside their ribcages or whether they are propelled by some remote control device in their garage. This assessment of the blasé attitude that the Leo/Ox emanates is perhaps harsh, or may seem unfair. But the Leo/Ox is so austere in manner that it's difficult not to imagine him as obdurately insensitive. Sexually, this person plumbs depths you or I could never even imagine if we tried. Despite an air of indifference, he or she will be sexually insatiable, but beware..."

LEO/TIGER – THE NOMADIC MANAGER

"The old Tiger admonition: "Seek temperance before it's too late". fits the Leo brand of Tiger to a T (as in Tiger). If moderation were to be ignored in this borderline arrogant character, the result would be: haughtiness in dissipation, disobedient self-satisfaction, swaggering tyranny. This is a tricky combination. The fate of an untempered Leo/Tiger could be disastrous. What this Tiger needs most it Love. But with his dashings about, leaping from activity to frenzy, Love sometimes eludes him. He needs to seek, find (and keep) a loving ally who can tuck him safely into bed and tickle his sexual fantasies which, believe me, are many and varied."

LEO/CAT-RABBIT – THE LOOPHOLE LEAPER

"This person is so nimble and quick-witted that to know him is to wonder where he went. The Leo/Cat is a double feline with all the evasiveness and slink that such a combination implies. Regal and independent, refined and endowed with Leo's noble generosity, this sort of person has the wherewithal for greatness. Yet. Leo/Cats rarely seek power or celebrity. Mostly they are content to sit home and listen to their money crinkle. The single character trait that prevents Leo/Cat from forging a public image is squeamishness. This person doesn't want to see the seamier side or life. He wants no part of bloodshed, conflict, confrontation or enmity. He is after a busy yet peaceful existence. The sex life of the Leo born Cat or Rabbit is as quiet and as regal as the rest."

LEO/DRAGON – THE MAGNIFICENT MAESTRO

"My notes on this combination proclaim: "A total egomaniac with a heart of gold." Is that what we are to think of Leo/Dragons? Are they truly so self-centered as to deserve the hyperbolic appellation of "egomaniac"? Yes. They are. But I mean it as a compliment. Very little stands in the way of this munificent leader's success. Yes. He or she longs for dominion over others. But these potential leaders are brainier than most, hence are not like to lead one over

the edge of a cliff. In their private lives, these folks aim for quality and usually don't settle for less in the bedroom. Sex is an important – nay - an essential part of this stunning creature's everyday life. Not easy to bed, he chooses partners carefully. But once upon that mattress, the Leo/Dragon delivers!"

LEO/SNAKE – THE SNAKE CHARMING

"The Snake born in Leo is always right. Even if he's wrong. He is nonetheless absolutely certain that he knows best. And frequently, especially for himself and in order to achieve his own ends, the Leo/Snake is not far off. Wisdom and clairvoyance are part of the Snake legacy. But the addition of Leo to the cool-headed Snake character, although it lends some sunshine and warmth, also deals this character a hand loaded with vanity. Now the already extravagant and presumptuous Snake has to carry around excess baggage in the form of a swollen skull that just doesn't quit. Love is the outlet that this person seeks – everywhere! Multiple love affairs, serial marriages and a deep longing for true love characterize this gorgeous person's sexual history. Intense lovemaking lends closeness and intimacy to this otherwise heady person's existence. Let's just say the Leo/Snake is famous for bone- chilling sexual exploits and, trust me, if you ever have the good fortune to bed one, you will remember my words..."

LEO/HORSE - THE POET CHAMPION

"This good-natured steed rides high among his fellows and practically always passes muster with flying colors. The Leo/Horse is a winner. He knows no obstacle too high nor does he fear adversity. This person wants more than anything in life to get there, to surpass himself in all areas of endeavor, and to do so in an atmosphere of good cheer. The Horse born Leo is not a sulker. His dauntless Leo side permits the normal fear of failure that haunts every Horse subject alive to retreat almost into oblivion. Sexually? Not surprisingly, this superlative person outperforms us all. He or she gives ample time and space to imaginative foreplay, then gets right down to the most erotic of..."

LEO/GOAT – THE WARRIOR ARTIST

"This Lion has the ephemeral spirit of an artist and the ambition of two Napoleon Bonapartes. It is just this mix of sensitivity and resolve that makes for the Leo/Goat's uncanny ability, despite fuzzy appearances and general lunacy, to arrive smack in the middle of the spotlight. Leo/Goats are blessed with the one thing most Goat people lack— common sense. They are both gentle and tough. This combination of sweetness and force carries over into the love life of this character who never ceases to amaze in the bedroom (as well as in the boardroom) with fancy new solutions to inspire pleasure in even the most reluctant of partners."

LEO/MONKEY - THE INSPIRED IMP

"The noble and magical Leo/Monkey is one beast you will never tire of learning about. This character has a heart of pure gold, a sterling silver tongue and a mind like a steel trap. He can tickle your funny bone. He will move you to tears. And if you hang around with him long enough, he may even drive you to drink. He's a powerful little devil whose imprint on everything and everyone he touches is indelible. You simply can't rub out the effects of this person's intricate actions. They are magnetic in the extreme. But not always world beaters. Effective in the sex department? Oh yeah. Count on this character to get right under the skin of his sexual partners."

LEO/ROOSTER – THE BRITTLE EGOIST

"The Rooster's many talents will invest this Leo subject with a wealth of choices unavailable to the normally undirected Leo person. Conversely, Roosters will benefit by being born with the noble, generous, magnanimous Leo aura. Where one of these signs is strong, the other tends to be lacking. Complementary indeed. Now, much as I like this person, I must confess he's bossy as hell. You toe the line. He makes the rules and you keep them. Yet, there is a whimsicality here too. This Rooster can be crack-you-up funny. But he is mostly serious and is especially loyal in love. Count on the Leo born Rooster for thrilling sexual experience."

LEO/DOG – THE NOBLE CAPTAIN

"All the Dog's respectability, heroism and undying constancy shot through with Leo loyalty, nobility and philanthropy find us confronted here with one of the most frankly earnest people ever born. So indulgent is this character with those he loves that if one of his friends committed a cold-blooded act of horror before his very eyes, the Leo/Dog would deny he saw it. He would find an excuse for the person. He would bake cake upon cake with files inside. He'd spring for the bail, the fines, the lawyers. And when finally, through his devoted efforts, his friend the criminal is set free again, Leo/Dog will find him a vacation spot, encourage his friend to invite whom he wants along and pick up the tab for that, too. Leo/Dogs are incorrigibly caring. And they are intelligent! They know how to get where they need to be to feel safe and keep things under control. These people are hyper sexy. No. I didn't say "oversexed". But almost. Despite a desire for lasting love in marriage, Leo/Dogs' sex lives are peppered with "shady' adventures and murky one night stands. It's the stray Dog thing which, despite Leo's nobility, rises once in awhile to the surface."

LEO/PIG – THE SYBARITIC JESTER

"This fiery, conscientious soul will always leave you laughing. Even in the most tragic circumstances, when the chips are down and Leo/Pigs seem to have reached an emotional nadir, from out the shivering bundle of despair will shine one little quip, one last pun or smart remark to bring a smile to your lips. Leo/Pigs cannot help it. They're funny people. It must be the Leo sun shining on the Pig's sincerity meter. Or else it s the Pig's honesty infused with Leo's philanthropic side. Whatever causes it, this person's sense of fun will be capital. As they are packed with emotion, they can also be super sad – even depressive. But they always pull out of their doldrums because these people simply adore living Life with a capital L. Experiencing natural pleasure is their most intimate aim. Food. Love. Children. Home. Countrysides etc. As they are both Leo and Pig. Sex is high on their list of priorities, I won't go into too much detail here because the juicy parts are a mite off color."

VIRGO

♍

VIRGO/RAT – THE SUPPORTIVE ANALYST

"A peppy, yet methodical person will be born of these two strong signs. Without the bulldozer punch of some of the other forceful New Astrological signs, the Virgo/Rat goes about his business craftily and with both system and industry. As both Virgo and Rat, he cannot help it. He wants to help others succeed. The Rat's aggressiveness is tempered here by Virgo's sober intelligence. Virgo/Rats are neither hotheaded nor foolish—except in love. Intimacy attracts them like bees to a bonnet. They are in love with being in love and will stop at nothing to find their heart's desire. Once they are steamed up about a sex partner, they go at it night and day, trying one position after the other to please – and to keep their lover enthralled and in bed."

VIRGO/OX – THE DISCRIMINATING HEAVYWEIGHT

"Nothing worthwhile ever comes easily," says the plodding model of human rectitude who is Virgo and Ox. An air of the ascetic emanates from this stolid character. He is deliberate. He is careful. He is meticulous. He is diligent, classical, traditionalist and sincere. And he never hangs out with anyone who is not at least some of the above. Virgo/Ox needs to rule his life single-handedly. He asks help of no one but his own people. These he has either hatched himself or chosen as friends and colleagues after much sorting and weeding out over the years. Loyal and true in both love and friendship, the Virgo born Ox wants, above all, to be seen to be steady at the helm. He or she enters the bedroom with a single goal in mind – well-oiled sex, engineered to satisfy even the most complex of partners. Short on imagination and long on lust."

VIRGO/TIGER – THE PRACTICAL SUNBEAM

"The Virgo/Tiger is a tough cookie with a heart of gold. These people don't let anything get past them. They notice and calculate and tot up and plan and pounce and re-tot up and re-pounce. It's an unbeatable combination for the person himself to live with, but maybe it's a little bit on the cranky, know-it-all side for those who have to live with him. Redeeming qualities? Plenty. But not necessarily in the sex department. Virgos born in Tiger years are lusty and make eager lovers. But they are also practical and hasty. They may be thinking about the schedule for the church picnic instead of focusing on their own sensuality. If I were writing a sexual report card for this rational genius, I would probably scribble, "Needs to concentrate" in the margin."

VIRGO/CAT-RABBIT – THE VIRTUOUS PUSSYFOOTER

"Virgo/Cat is the picture of caution. His first portrait can only be painted after many years of slow and deliberate development. You will never hear him complain, nor will you notice him creeping up on you. This person is sagaciously circumspect, stays out of the way of danger and will even throw away what is most important to him just to keep the peace and dodge conflict. Effective? You bet he is. Make no mistake. Just because the Virgo/Cat is discreet and refined, doesn't mean he can't get plenty done behind the scenes. He flees conflict. Then he works behind the scenes to accomplish great good works. In the bedroom this person is just the pussycat he or she appears to be. Cuddling and affection mean a lot to this creature of comfort. Seduce and nuzzle before use."

VIRGO/DRAGON – THE COOL NIT PICKER

"The Virgo/Dragon couples Virgo decorum with Dragon sizzle. This Dragon is hard-edged. He has enough spunk and perseverance to take a dare to walk across Australia – solo! He always maintains a coy Virgo reserve in order to keep Dragonish taste for fresh blood under dignified wraps. If you're looking for performance, it's a hard to beat combination. The fiery Dragonesque soul is tempered by Virgo's taste for social grace. Virgo/Dragon is ambitious and has a mind like a platinum bear trap. The sex life of a Dragon born in Virgo has two parts. In youth, it is kinky and weird. This character has a murky side and might indulge in all manner of zany sex practices while young. But after age 30, they reach their cruising altitude and wallow in the safety of luscious (but private) domestic sex."

VIRGO/SNAKE – THE DETACHED OBSERVER

"Analysis and intuition are two essential elements in the personality of a Virgo/Snake. This Virgo is both emotional and attractive. He is endowed with wisdom and depth of understanding. He may appear serious and even grave. The tongue, you will notice, however, is conveniently stored inside the cheek. This person's strength is that he is not really of the world. Virgo/Snakes exist outside of the mundane and always wear a secret smile. Sex and the Snake go together. Being born in sensible Virgo may make this Snake a tad less lascivious than his or her counterparts. But bottom line, this person is always looking for love. Real pure honest affection turns him or her on more than any other kind of seduction tactic. If you find yourself in bed with this perceptive soul, don't be surprised at the variety of intricate techniques he or she uses."

VIRGO/HORSE – THE PRANCING PRODUCER

"The marriage of Virgo and Horse is one both lofty and elegant. Horses are self-motivated strivers, doers of grand deeds and sometimes—with all of their parading—a mite foolish and overly passionate. The Virgo, as we all know by now, is reserved. He takes care never to go outside the lines in the coloring book of life. Virgo is tasteful and a bit of a nit-picker to boot. He or she is also a borderline social climber. You won't find this subject hiding under any rocks or living among the homeless. His associations as well as his goals are high-minded and often intellectual. The Love life of the Virgo born Horse is never dull. He is both amiable and appealing. People literally fall at this alluring person's feet. In bed, he will be efficient – not cuddly or cozy – but effective and eager to achieve satisfaction by any and all means available. If ever you find yourself in bed with this entrancing creature, you might be shocked. But you won't be surprised at the skill."

VIRGO/GOAT – THE VERBOSE ODDBALL

The combination of the purity and crackle of Virgo with Goat dependency and love of luxury make for a rather uncertain personality type. This person's sturdy Virgo side wants to come across as a serious and efficacious worker. He bolsters his image so as to better believe in himself. But the languor-loving Goat invariably comes gamboling along and tips Virgo's rigidity right over. What we get then is a person with very strong opinions who is easily influenced and prey to those more crafty and less gullible than himself. The love and sex patterns in this oddball's life are unusually checkered. It's difficult for the Virgo born Goat to decide what it is he or she precisely wants in a sex partner. So they try many different ones, sample each for a while and then move on. This method of finding an ideal couple in which to thrive and grow, is, of course, hellishly unreliable. If you get yourself intimately involved with this character, you will be amazed the variety of techniques he or she has picked up along the way. Don't expect marriage proposals... just have fun."

VIRGO/MONKEY – THE CUNNING PERFECTIONIST

The Virgo born Monkey carries himself like a prince. Women of this sign are elegant and stunning to behold. They give off the kind of superior vibes equaled only by the wicked queen in Disney's Snow White. Nonetheless, Virgo/Monkeys never have it easy. They must nibble away at all aspects of their lives, from childhood onward, in order to enjoy even a measure of success. Why? Because Virgos born in Monkey years are conflicted. Virgo wants social status. Monkey doesn't care a fig whether he belongs to the right clubs or rubs shoulders with prominent people. Goals are never quite clear to this clever character. Success is sometimes considered a mixed blessing. But never mind because the best thing the Virgo/Monkey knows how to do is make money and keep it. In love, he is sentimental, possessive and even a mite clingy. Naturally this makes him a top notch, competent lover with techniques and skills hitherto unimagined by less meticulously driven romantics..."

VIRGO/ROOSTER – THE ELEGANT INDIVIDUALIST

"This brand of Rooster keeps coming back for more and rising victorious from even the muddiest miasma, or else he dies trying. Virgo and Rooster are signs of determination and pluck. There is a truckload of perseverance here. These people are drivers whose love of detail and acuity for fact-gathering make them useful to society as well as to themselves. And where I say society, I mean Society. The Virgo born Rooster wants his or her place in the social stratum to be well defined and will labor diligently and long to get to belong to the right clubs and drive the best cars and live in relative luxury. His or her love style is rather less passionate than that of many other (cockier) Roosters. The Virgo side of this person wants to maintain decorum and so never dives headlong into bed with "just anybody". Once in bed however, this subject can be counted on to perform all lovemaking vigorously and with much imagination."

VIRGO/DOG – THE HANDSOME BENEFACTOR

Kindness and bite combine in the Virgo/Dog character. No matter how crabby this person may seem at times, a vigil light of sweetness burns brightly from behind his eyes. Virgo/Dogs may try to hide their vulnerability under a cloak of sophistication and worldliness. But beneath the veneer is a surface as sensitive and soft as purest down. Virgo/Dogs are reliable people who practice good works. You can always call on one of these charitable folks for assistance in times of need. Their private lives often remain discreetly hidden. But, if you have the good fortune to find yourself in a compromising position with one of these very beautiful people, you will be surprised at the sexual energy behind the sometimes austere façade. Even though they are among the most attractive people alive, Virgo/Dogs are, after all, still Dogs."

VIRGO/PIG –THE BOHEMIAN PURIST

"For the Virgo/Pig, wickedness doesn't really exist. These people really don't think that base, low, crafty, evil souls are dancing about our ears at all times in all climes. Virgo/Pig is born believing in the noble savage. To him, all people, animals and even inanimate objects are basically right and honorable. They may err. Oh yes, people or animals may stray from the path of righteousness. But it is always the fault of society. The Virgo born Pig is often a crusader - an advocate for the underdog or a champion of the misunderstood. He or she may possess a gypsy-like quality and often revel in playing the bohemian. But behind the scenes, this person's lifestyle borders on lavish. The sexuality of these idealistic subjects will be somewhat reserved and his or her selection of bed partners on the "choosy" side."

http://suzannewhite.com/astrology/newAstrology.html

Visit **http://suzannewhite.com** for Personal Chart Readings
Books, Horoscopes & Lifestyle Advice

LIBRA

♎

LIBRA/RAT – THE STRIVING RACONTEUR

"A gifted combination, the Libra/Rat lives in a perpetual state of hopefulness. He or she wants to break the bank at Monte Carlo, star in a play on Broadway and... write a bestseller. Further, they'd like to beget—or better still, be— the president of the United States. And when she is finished with those incidentals, she would like to take time out to win the Nobel Prize. Libra/Rats are almost self-destructively ambitious. Their truest gifts lie within the realms of poetry and fantasy. These people are exhaustingly communicative. They want to tell it all, all the time and in the most excruciating detail. To know them is to love them. But keep your eye peeled for little fault lines. Because there are some. Libra/Rats are feverishly sensitive and can "dish it out but can't take it". They can be cutting to others. But wilt when spoken to harshly. Their private lives are fraught with emotional booby traps. If you find yourself in love with a Libra/Rat, take him or her directly to bed. Very good value in the sack means..."

LIBRA/OX – THE LUCID SEEKER

"Beauty and the Beast. This subject is a veritable storm of contradiction. Every detail must be perfect, every line straight and every flaw concealed. Weakness must be routed. Sloth eradicated. Yet, under this foil of faultlessness, Libra/Ox hides a secret. On the strict surface, Libra/Ox is efficiency and power, example and security. Underneath? An anthill of conflicting emotions. Purity charms this sterling character. He claims not to want any messes about. He protests he needs calm and cannot live in turmoil, Yet, Libra/Oxen are forever getting themselves involved in emotional scrapes. Even though they seem to be above it all, they take in strays. They seek out madness. They are magnetized by complexity. The love life of Librans born in Ox year roil with complications. Nothing is simple – even in the bedroom where arcane tactics and multiple fantasies..."

LIBRA/TIGER - THE GENTEEL REVOLUTIONARY

An original if there ever was one, the Libra/Tiger is unforgettably winning. This person wants to impress and please you. You will warm to the Tigerish Libran charisma and want to know more—much more—about him. Attractive? My gawd. These people emit personal magnetism rays that dance all over their countenances. Libra/Tiger seems perpetually on the brink of bursting out laughing. It's adorable. It's fascinating. And it is mighty perilous for the heartstrings. Should you have the good fortune to find yourself entwined with this tawny beast in his or her musky lair, lie back and enjoy the fun. Libra/Tiger sex is seriously naughty. Mammoth imagination goes into every smooch and caress ..."

LIBRA/CAT-RABBIT – THE DIPLOMATIC ENIGMA

"Tasteful, safe and gracious living is the aim of the character born in the double sign of aesthetic appreciation. Librans born in Cat years are stay-at-home, suspicious, squeamish souls. They trust with great difficulty. Libra's discretion about passing quick judgments becomes, in this subject, a near refusal to judge anything or anyone. Libra/Cats hesitate so long before making decisions or committing themselves that they frequently lose their prey. These subjects are, however, socially conscious. They worry endlessly about the fate of the underdog and long to improve the lot of everyone in the universe. Trouble is, they want the universe to cooperate, to see things their way and will argue vehemently if the universe doesn't comply. The intimate life of Libra/Cats is intricate. Romantic entanglement fascinates them."

LIBRA/DRAGON – THE INVITING CELEBRITY

"The Libra/Dragon is not just anybody. Librans are born manipulators. Dragons tend to be suspicious. Librans seek equilibrium in all matters. Dragons seek to be heard and seen. Neither sign is particularly taciturn. The match is stormy. But despite the tempestuous nature of the Libra/Dragon, he or she will be gifted in carving out unusual destinies. Nobody much trifles with the feelings of this monster of taste and talent. His or her charismatic presence is sought after by all manner of people he or she seduces somehow just by being there. To succeed at being the mate of this huge soul, one must know how to applaud even when the music is not that great or the artwork just so-so. Thanks to this highly attractive person's wild imagination, Libra born Dragon lovemaking may be slightly kinky and certainly memorable."

LIBRA/SNAKE - THE ENCHANTING CRUSADER

"Magnetism personified. The Libra born in a Snake year will, above all, attract. This combination is a mostly happy one. People born under this sign may be less so. This is because they are not only irresistible; they are also stubborn and willful. They want things done their way, and like to order others around subtly. Often, things are done for them, their way, by willing lackeys. These people have charisma to burn. Libran Snakes rule others through emotion. They are capable of sensing exactly what another needs from them. They are remarkably perceptive and even have a gift for the supernatural. Librans born in Snake years know how to exalt an audience with their cool, reasonable yet emphatically sentimental discourse. These people are born to serve as shepherds of human flocks, moralizers and brotherhood mongers. In private, they are all love, sensuality, sexiness and grand romance. Too gorgeous to be forever faithful, they still make marvelous mates. Libra/Snake sex is luscious, intimate and slightly other worldly."

LIBRA/HORSE – THE MEASURED COMMANDER

"A Horse born in gracious Libra will be genteel and dignified. Horses are sometimes rebellious and hardheaded. Libra practically never is. Libra wants peace and knows how to go after equilibrium. In this sign, Libra climbs on to the Horse's back and hangs on for dear life until she has tamed the selfish stallion into a better, more civilized person. When joined to Libra, the Horse retains full interest in his elegance and style. He hangs on tight to popularity and has the market cornered on idealism. Libra lends the Horse refined taste. Libra knows that with her well-developed sense of measure the Horse will never totally buck the system. Passion is more important than tenderness in the love life of this person. Intimacy with a Libra/Horse is guaranteed bliss between the sheets."

LIBRA/GOAT – THE CONTENTIOUS FLIRT

"Ostensibly a dependent lover of beauty and equilibrium, this person claims to need a peaceful environment, but we know better. Librans born in Goat years are testy and quarrelsome people. They love an argument, a good old heated discussion, and a challenge. The Libra/Goat requires the regard of his peers. He likes to be looked at, contemplated, taken seriously and admired. To this end, the Libra/Goat will do almost anything—once. Libra/Goats are bit lightheaded; but they are not superficial. They can work intensely and long to reach a goal and often bite off a lot more than it seems they will be able to chew. Admire a Libra/Goat and they will follow you anywhere.

Romance is one area where these folks really shine! Candlelight dinners, trips to tropical paradises, downy four-poster beds and lacy underwear merely foreplay. Sex is omnipresent in this sensual person's life. He or she knows precisely what to do."

LIBRA/MONKEY – THE GLIB MANIPULATOR

"The Libra side of this person's nature will want to live life as a couple and will be attracted to early marriage. Adding Monkey traits to the jabbery Libra's chart infuses it with an increased need for communication—and even a certain desire for healthy conflict. The Libra/Monkey combo is not restful. These people are attracted to motion for its own sake. Sometimes they need to forget what they have just seen and travel on to new territories in order to soak up some joyful or at least different vibrations. Love, for the Libra/Monkey, must sizzle and snap. No lukewarm one night stands for this highly evolved gourmet of passion. Because they remain youthful well into old age, Librans born in Monkey years are not always lifelong faithful to one partner. But while they are being held in thrall by a lover, they are skilled and tender with techniques."

LIBRA/ROOSTER – THE ZESTY INDEPENDENT

"Rooster often lives a life full of chasms of despair followed by summits of felicity. And thank Zeus for Libra's sense of equilibrium. Libra lends poetry to the Rooster's cocky strictness and tickles his conservatism, even prodding it into the occasional flight of fancy. Also, Libra tempers the Rooster's tendency to overreact. For a Rooster, this person will be gentle and might even qualify as "calm." The Rooster brings energy and candor the laid back Libra creating a character with an unusual spunky charm. There is something almost liquid about the Libra/Rooster's gaze. He is deep-thinking and innovative and will likely maintain a lifelong love relationship. Plenty of spirit and laughter in the bedroom make this character an enticing lover partner."

LIBRA/DOG –THE SNAPPISH MEDIATOR

"Libra/Dogs are both dignified and brilliant. They possess innate humanitarianism and are softhearted in the best possible way. You will always be able to get sympathy from a Libra/Dog. He will help you, cheer you along and applaud your courage. He's a great friend, a super associate and a bundle of nerves. Libra is able to sort out any of life's conflicts through diplomacy and impartiality. In fact, one of the most annoying things about Libras is their refusal to take unpopular stands. They can always see both sides and will often agree with an adversary merely to keep the peace. This is a gentle (if sometimes controlling) soul with a brusque manner and a biting tongue who basically wouldn't hurt a flea. Love and the Libra/Dog? Loyal. True. Faithful... and mostly very naughty in bed!"

LIBRA/PIG – THE ARDENT CURATOR

"Loving is what the Libra/Pig does best. This person is devoted, exclusive, jealous and loyal. Nothing really counts much in the Libran Pig's life except the relationship he or she has with a mate, child, sibling or parent. All activity centers around the bond that Libra/Pig has created with someone else. Professions, money, children, hobbies, friendships—you name it—will be relegated to second place. Libra/Pigs are artistic homebodies who excel at crafts and glory in building things with their hands. In Love? Nothing can ever get in the way of this person's drive for first place in the heart of a beloved mate. The Libra born Pig loves with an intense exclusivity that borders on paranoia. If you happen to fall into the happy clutches of one of these obliging, adoring creatures, consider yourself lucky. But don't try anything extramarital – not even a night out with the boys/girls. Sexuality? Fabulous. And willing."

SCORPIO

♏

SCORPIO/RAT – THE DESIGNING MASTERMIND

"A sharp-tongued, wily magpie if ever there was one, the Scorpio born in a Rat year will be chatty and cutting. This person is generally lithe and agile as well as quick-spirited. He or she will probably enjoy all manner of graceful sport and prove able at competitive games. The Scorpio/Rat is an amiable fellow. People like him or her straight away and never guess that behind the ready smile is a rare drive for power. He wants to hold the most potent place in whatever area he has chosen as his own. This Rat's private life is often fraught with betrayal. Like other Rats, the Scorpio born is the marrying kind. But his marriages sometimes collapse of their own weight as he is highly sensual and apt to get into some very wicked sexual mischief."

SCORPIO/OX - THE BEMUSED BEHEMOTH

"A whiz kid with a crazy streak is the Scorpio born in Ox years. Oxen are deliberate, plain people who, as a rule, stodge their way to success come hell or high water. Scorpios are tricky and fanatical, mistrustful and magnetic. They veer all over the place in order to attain goals that the lumbering Ox heads for, horns lowered, steady as you plod. Put these two signs together and you get a kind of zippy Kremlin or a slightly kooky Sherman tank. Scorpio/Oxen are always on their way somewhere. Never in a hurry—oh no. They are simply ruthlessly and sadistically determined to get where they are going, which is usually to the top of the profession where there are the highest salaries and the most glory, seniority and prestige. The love lives of these heavy hitters are passionate and fiery. But they do not always supply the passion or the fire. People simply fall hopelessly in love with them and once they get them into bed, can never again extinguish the flames of desire."

SCORPIO/TIGER – THE LIFE GUZZLER

"Scorpio/Tigers are excessive. They do everything to extreme. They never take life as it comes, but rather race out and try to head it off at the pass. They are constantly in dangerous situations, where they have plunked themselves deliberately. They never take their time and plan every detail, or write lists to be sure that every last mothball gets accounted for in the winter clothes. These people are hasty and hotheaded and really honestly quite mad. I call Scorpio/Tigers "blitz" people. They come screeching up to every new experience, gobble, slurp, inhale, consume, build, make, bake, scrape, paint, fix—and they're off to the next challenge. Scorpios born in Tiger years are always trying to get three lives out of one. Want to know more about the lusty sex lives of these gourmet bon vivants? That's easy. For a Scorpio born Tiger, more is definitely not less. More is more and more is better. These people need sex and the satisfactions of same, the way snow needs cold to survive. Affectionate and loving and even mostly faithful (as long as the sex is good), these people will try anything - and not just once or twice either."

SCORPIO/CAT-RABBIT - THE DEVOUT REFORMER

"When a Scorpio is born in a Cat/Rabbit year, he's almost as tough as a Tiger. An imposing figure is the Scorpio/Cat. He is admirable, well able to earn and keep his money and command respect from peers. On the outside, he is calm and refined. On the inside there's a blazing fire of intent. Scorpio/Cat means what he says and says only what he means. He's thought it all through beforehand and believes fervently in whatever theories or precepts he is advancing. This character is not a person to be taken lightly. She will need to see her work or project or ideal come to fruition and will work night and day to make that happen satisfactorily. Not one to treat love superficially, this person usually chooses a life partner early on, marries and make a comfortable home for his family. His sex life will be adequate, but spouses and kids have to take second place to this person's mission in life. In sexual situations, the Scorpio/Cat/Rabbit will perform handsomely."

SCORPIO/DRAGON – THE FIERCE ENCHANTER

"When you add Dragon to Scorpio and mix well to blend, the batter thickens and fizzes up and oozes over the sides of the bowl. This combo is BIG. Scorpio lends mystery and ruthlessness to an already plucky and boastful Dragon nature. Add a dash of swagger and some good old Scorpio vengeance and jealousy and you will concoct yourself a mighty baroque human being. This dish is spicy and copious and never lets up on the desire to win and keep on winning. In life in general, the Dragon born Scorpio usually takes over any group he or she belongs to. But, as they prefer to fly solo, they don't join many groups. Loners and leaders are made of this stuff. They handle their professional lives as skillfully as they do their very busy (and crowded) sex lives. Being in bed with a Scorpio/Dragon is anything but restful. These creatures need plenty of burning, passionate sexual activity and they almost always take the lead."

SCORPIO/SNAKE – THE LUXURIANT PHILOSOPHER

"To a Scorpio/Snake, life without beauty and luxury, tenderness, compassion, admiration and extravagance is not worth living. This person is sensitive in the extreme and, for a cool-handed Snake, remarkably warm-hearted and loving. People appreciate this character for a certain innate nobility, which is both unquestionable and very comforting. Scorpios are already very sensual people with a tendency to introspect and suspect. To add the Snake characteristics of sagacity, clairvoyance and intuition certainly doesn't diminish the philosophical side of Scorpio's nature. This person is deep-thinking, sometimes even tormented. The love life of a Scorpio born Snake is always compelling. They take on lovers and acquire spouses, as effortlessly as they splurge on luxury items at every airport duty free shop. Scorpios born in Snake years enter love affairs with a dense silent passion. Then. Sometime later, their utterly rambunctious, noisy plate-throwing breakups go clattering about the newspapers and gossip columns of the world and we wonder whatever happened to that nice dense quiet passion. Let's just say this person is a sexual powerhouse whose grip on his or her lovers tends to be at least ruthless, if not lethal."

SCORPIO/HORSE – THE ROUGHSHOD PLODDER

"This creature embodies most of the positive traits of the signs it combines. Scorpio/Horses are magnetic. And they are popular. They are disciplined and accomplished. They are persuasive and inspired, dedicated and fashionable. Scorpios born in Horse years are both independent and autonomous. There is little to prevent these folks from succeeding in a world class way. However, these strong-minded, sassy individuals are "can-do" people with immense personal power. Woe unto the associate who is not just as capable. Scorpio/Horse has no patience for lily-livered laggards. He rides himself hard and expects the same of partners and employees. Ironically, these feisty people love to do good works, assist the poor and heal the unwashed. Go figure. This is a hard sign to live with – for both the person wearing it and his or her entourage.

Faithful in love (they ought to be cuz they ain't easy) the Scorpio/Horse adores his family, works overtime to protect and care for them and makes love like there was no tomorrow."

SCORPIO/GOAT – THE DEXTEROUS MAGICIAN

"Scorpio/Goats tend to live off the endeavors of others. By this, I certainly don't mean that they refuse to work on their own. Far from it. But their choice of work is invariably dependent on a structure coming from without. They are not gifted with inner discipline. And that's okay because their genius overrides the need for order. Once they have established their brilliance as a given, they can set about getting their lives structured by outside forces. This force can take the form of a marriage, a business, a child or two, a project, a course of study or even a lover or mistress. The Goat born in Scorpio is one of the luckiest Goats because the Scorpio lends enormous pluck and sensuality to an already massively creative Goat. In Love, this person is loyal and true. Sex is however what makes him and keeps him that way. If you long for a quiet sex life, stay away from these hyper sexual people."

SCORPIO/MONKEY – THE EFFERVESCENT SMOOTHIE

"Combining plotting and creativity can cause some human fireworks. The Scorpio born in a Monkey year will bear all the earmarks of the complex Scorpio nature. He will be crafty and enigmatic and harsh-tongued and strong. Yet he will seek to muffle those darker characteristics by pretending jauntiness and affecting a slightly silly attitude at times. Monkey and Scorpio can sometimes be—but only sometimes—allies. They are both tricky and ruseful. They are both capable of leadership. At other times, however, these two signs are at odds. Monkeys are sometimes deceitful but pretend they are only kidding around. Scorpio is hardly ever just fooling around. Scorpio means business. Monkeys are builders. Scorpios can be destroyers. Monkeys are zealous, Scorpios jealous. But never mind. These characters make exciting lovers. They are active in the extreme and cook up all manner of thrilling sexploits with their willing partners. Faithful? Don't count on it."

SCORPIO/ROOSTER – THE OBEDIENT REBEL

"Talent is no stranger to the Rooster born a Scorpio. This person usually has bushels of skills. Scorpio/Roosters are idealists and, because of the crossing of Scorpio's determination with the Rooster's resilience, will suffer less from setbacks than many other people. The Scorpio/Rooster's story is invariably one of climbing precipitous summits followed by full fanny slides back down. The craggy chasms in which you sometimes find Scorpio/Roosters flailing about seem not to ruffle their feathers. It's amazing how they bounce back from sorrow, divorce, loss and human bankruptcies of all sorts. These people seem fragile, almost brittle at times. But they are really solid and strong. If the Scorpio/Rooster doesn't meet the love of his life and settle down as a happy couple, his romantic picture can look like a bad train wreck. He is not keen on flailing about in the muddy waters of casual sexual escapades."

SCORPIO/DOG – THE SNAPPISH HUMANIST

"Both Scorpio and Dog are dedicated and devoted. Scorpio lends fire to this dedication, and if betrayed, adds jealousy as well. Both Dogs and Scorpios like to advance strong opinions. Dog is a shade more know-it-all than the secretive Scorpio. But Scorpio can hold his own in conversation. And Dogs do a lot of nipping and snapping. With the Scorpio's viper tongue to dispatch the Dog's verbal snipes, you can readily see that this is not a person who minces words. The Scorpio/Dog character is acerbic and sarcastic. Yet, at the same time he or she can be very kindly and full of brotherly love. If riled however, (and that is not difficult with this edgy soul), the Scorpio/Dog can be sadistic in his commentary. Let's just say that the Scorpio/Dog uses his tongue and his wits to battle his way through life. This character has no use for disappointment in love. Once burned. Twice shy. He or she is a fervent sexual partner who gives value in return for devotion. Not easy to seduce. But worth it."

SCORPIO/PIG – THE ADMIRABLE SEDUCER

"In his book Animal Farm, George Orwell writes in jest that "all pigs are created equal... but some are more equal than others." The Scorpio/Pig possesses natural magnificence. He's duskier than most Pigs. Scorpio has just what the doctor ordered to remedy that silly piggie credulity: suspicion. It's a good match. This person will surely go a long way in life. Moreover, he or she will be cheered along by many admiring companions. Often, Scorpios born in Pig years are exceptionally good-looking. They have an enigmatic quality that other more direct Pigs would envy. What's more, Scorpio/Pigs know how to dress. Both signs have a taste for the sensually appealing. Watch for elegant décolletages and spiffy smoking jackets. Sex and power are the special provinces of the Scorpio born Pig. These folks wallow in intrigue and often use their sex appeal to win out against fearsome foes. Sensuality oozes out this Pig's very pores."

SAGITTARIUS

♐

SAGITTARIUS/RAT - THE DIRECT HITTER

"The marriage of Sagittarius to Rat brings us a vivacious person brimming with energy, adventure and activity. The Sagittarius born Rat just about never sits still. This person likes groups and is often surrounded by guests, friends and family. Less charm-conscious than many Rat subjects, the Sagittarian is impatient to achieve and is not concerned about what others think of him. He or she presents a candid self-image without frills or pretense. If you like that sort of thing, you will enjoy this dynamic Sagittarian's company. If you are not attracted by his or her simplicity and directness, then you don't have to come around. It's all the same to Sagittarius/Rat. He has no time to waste pleasing dissenters. This character is built for doing business and making money at it. Love? Well the Sag/Rat wants sex. But he or she quite independent and picky about with whom. Once they locate the partner of their dreams., they go at sex as though they had been starved for it -and often (because of their super charged professional endeavors) they have been. If you are lucky enough to bed one these sexual dynamos, please don't complain about how exhausted you are the next morning."

SAGITTARIUS/OX - THE HUMAN SNOWPLOW

"Oxen can really accomplish a lot in life. But Sagittarius/Oxen can do more. These folks are super charged bulldozer people. They are both fiery and placid. They are eloquent fast talkers too. They are direct, humanistic, openhanded and strong. What's more, Sagittarians born in Ox years are ambitious for power, influence, control and prestige. They don't despise money, either. What's most surprising about the Sagittarian/Ox is his or her perseverance. This creature gloms onto a project and sticks with it - against all odds - until the job is done. Not very tolerant of slug-a- beds or lazies, this person will be a demanding boss who routinely accomplished more than any employee. There is little this character cannot do. When young, the Sag/Ox is often busy flitting about seeking a life partner. He or she will have a firm idea of the type he or she needs to make him happy. Once he settles with a partner for life, this character paints a lusty sexual picture, complete with gadgetry."

SAGITTARIUS/TIGER - THE IMPULSIVE PACESETTER

"The Sagittarius born Tiger is a person who stubbornly, but charmingly, wishes to remain a child. These people love all the trappings of adventure and toys, exciting new technologies and long journeys to faraway lands. Of course, children cannot realize such dramatic dreams. They only imagine what it's like to ride in a space ship or dive thousands of feet into the ocean's depths. So Sagittarius/Tiger kids (and adults) will fantasize about great adventures. But they rarely go further than their own backyards. Oh, yes, they will take long walks into the mountains, discover ruins and memorize each stone. But these very dear, funny people never leave home for long. Late bloomers, their taste for exploration does eventually get them started on a journey toward success. This type can start small, work hard and excel easily at what he does. His love life is chockablock with ups and downs. He likes sex. But he's not going to settle easily with one person. His early life a full of sexploits and short-lived affairs. Once he finds the right person, however, he will marry, have plenty of kids (to play with) and engage his regular sexual partner in some very musky games."

SAGITTARIUS/CAT-RABBIT - THE ASTUTE GO GETTER

"The prudent Cat side of this couple tugs at the Sagittarian's carefree arrow till he snaps it loose. It falls to the ground before leaving the bow. In words, in this person the recklessness of Sagittarius is defused by the Cat's virtue and sense of measure. This Sagittarian is not quite so brash as his brothers and sisters. A Sagittarian born in a Cat year senses his real surroundings. He has radar awareness of the need for diplomacy and, because of the Cat's serious ambition, may be sagaciously yoked to his or her career. These people are often performers or musicians or artists as well. The fiery Sagittarian slows down long enough under the Cat/Rabbit's influence to pursue a dream. The love life of a Sag/Cat/Rabbit is never built on a flat plain where a family grows placidly like a happy field of mushrooms. There is so much verve and sexual drive here that practically nobody can ever keep up the pace. As a result, marriages can be hasty and short-lived. Sex oozes from this person's seductive nature."

SAGITTARIUS/DRAGON - THE GENTLEMAN VICTOR

"An admirable but not always gentle character, the Sagittarius/Dragon is a warrior on the grand scale. These people are attractive and ambitious. They believe in success and forge ahead with bravura toward that aim. Never bullish or hotheaded, this character's style is gentlemanly and dignified. Sagittarius/Dragons are not afraid of danger. They take great risks and even court peril. They dance around the flame of adventure and derring-do but they rarely get seriously burned. Dragons born in Sagittarius outwit their enemies, hoist them on their own petards and invite them to lunch the next day. Victory, after all, calls for a celebration. Nobody can match this fire-breathing powerhouse in the bedroom. Being sentimental, he or she makes much of marriage and proves an excellent parent. He likes a busy life, crowded with kin and festivity. These crowds are never invited to the bedroom. The Sag/Dragon is an arch romantic. A thousand candles lit in honor of one sexual exploit could never be enough."

SAGITTARIUS/SNAKE - THE CONSIDERATE CARETAKER

"Solicitude personified, the Sagittarius/Snake cares for those he loves and admires, and looks after everything from home to car interior with a sense of concern that makes Florence Nightingale look like a slouch. This is a creature of dignity and bearing whose manners and taste for refinement are second only to an unparalleled devotion to virtue. The Sagittarian Snake is a human luxury item, without the expensive price tag. It's odd just how daringly this person goes after what he or she wants - and most times gets it. Born with an almost superhuman high opinion of their own abilities (which are superior indeed), Sagittarians born in Snake years are always working to improve on what is: build a better mouse trap, find a new way to house orphans, invent a method for detoxifying the air in hospitals. This character is known for marrying late - or not at all. This does not mean they don't have rich sex lives. The Sag/Snake is almost too attractive and has lovers and mistresses galore."

SAGITTARIUS/HORSE - THE KINDLY SPECULATOR

"A great striding Horse figure, the Sagittarius/Horse is three-quarters Horse and only one part man. As they say in westerns, "That's a lot of horse!" Interestingly, this person is more head than beast. The Sagittarian born Horse operates first out of homespun values, next in search of self-control, and thirdly he concentrates on finding and achieving a goal. Despite being born an adventurous Sagittarian, there is something of the plodder about this Horse. He's conventional and likes everything to "look good" on the surface. This is a practical person first, a romantic second. He marries and settles. But often leads a checkered double life in a quest for something a bit raunchier than just routine sex. This person's sexual prowess is legendary among her occasional partners. But her husband may not know about the seamier side."

SAGITTARIUS/GOAT – THE STYLISH ADVENTURER

"Sagittarius/Goat enjoys a giant creativity. Invention and enterprise are second nature to this dynamic, clear-thinking soul. Yet, there is one rub. Goats only function well when they feel secure. Lack of means or the threat of financial ruin, family schisms and personal jeopardizes of all sorts will flummox this Goat and throw him off his feed. The major struggle for this valiant and courageous character will revolve around getting and keeping protection for himself and family and friends. He or she spends time in the early part of his life seeking security. Until he has amassed sufficient means to provide for a family, he may not settle down at all. Adventures? Sexual affairs? Oh yeah. Lots."

SAGITTARIUS/MONKEY – THE GAMBLING TRAILBLAZER

"Sagittarians are always freethinkers. They blaze trails and shoot for the future. They are glib and humanitarian. They are direct and cheerful. Much of the above description also fits the Monkey character. So, in some ways, the Sagittarian Monkey is in harmony with both sides of his nature. His outgoing side doesn't have to do daily battle with some introverted tendency to hide under rocks when company comes. Sagittarius/Monkey is mostly comfortable in his skin. And he is a gambler. Working out problems, which mystify others, delights this Byzantine character. He or she is constantly searching for a way to break the bank at Monte Carlo - a system for beating the system. The Sagittarian/Monkey is also a rover. Look for this creature selling real estate in darkest Africa or peddling sophisticated ice cream makers in Siberia. Challenge - but oddball challenge - is what they are all about. Love and sex? These folks seem to have ton of both in their busy lives at all times. How do they do it? Well."

SAGITTARIUS/ROOSTER - THE CHATTY ENTHUSIAST

Buoyancy characterizes the Sagittarian Rooster. He's atwitter with chitchat and agog with stories of adventure. This subject, born under two of the most high-strung signs, will be nervous, frank, candid, and a bit carried away with himself. The word is enthusiasm but it's more than that. Sagittarius/Roosters are full of dash and élan. They cut an impressive figure wherever they go—and they go everywhere! Superficially, this character appears boastful and cocky. But deep down he is serious, dreams of helping the downtrodden and cares enormously about others. His love life is highly charged, but uneven. Great passions come alive and carry him to heavenly heights. The next week, it's over. The paradox lies in this person's odd relationship to deceit. He can't stand untruth and yet is capable of some devious fibbing of his own. This approach makes cementing love into anything more permanent than a roll in the hay in a grass hut. The sex is surely delicious. But don't count on this character to still be there in the morning."

SAGITTARIUS/DOG - THE WORTHY KNIGHT

The dry hero that is Sagittarius/Dog embodies all of the Sagittarian's idealist traits, the adventurousness, the future vision, the bravura and the fire. But this person also takes on those creditable qualities native to all born under the sign of the Dog: honor and sincerity, loyalty and respectability. Both signs are endowed with a loose tongue. Sagittarians like to be frank and to expound. Dogs, although circumspect and mistrustful, tend to lash out with words, toppling adversaries like tenpins. This is a worthy person whose nose for what's happening on the world scene and how to fix it is enviably accurate. You will often find these people in the medical or healing professions. They can't help wanting to help others, improve their lot, comfort their sorrows. The private lives of these people are very private indeed. They are extremely sexual. But never air their dirty linen or kiss and tell about this or that affair."

SAGITTARIUS/PIG - THE HONORABLE SENSUALIST

"Still waters run deep. The Sagittarian Pig, above reproach in moral conduct and beyond social disapprobation, tries very hard to maintain a spotless reputation. Not that the Sagittarius/Pig is a Pollyanna and only capable of Boy Scoutism. Not at all. But this person attends to his or her public name by staying clear of trouble and acting the role of moralist. Of course, this pristine do-good behavior only goes so far. The Sagittarian/Pig is still (pardon the expression) a Pig. So this upstanding citizen type who has many axes to grind with everything from politics to artistic expression is frequently found out to be a secret wallower."

http://suzannewhite.com/astrology/newAstrology.html

CAPRICORN

♑

CAPRICORN/RAT - THE DILIGENT CLIMBER

"Both Capricorn and Rat want to achieve success. Rat wants power. Capricorn wants sway over others. Together the covetous Rat and the solitary mountain goat that is Capricorn will go far (many times to the detriment of anything from reputation to family or even health). The Capricorn born Rat, like the Tiger only more so, is in constant, grievous danger. Why? Because this person is a Rat and so is ambitious for power. Moreover, he's a slow-moving solitary Capricorn whose unshod hooves climb the mountain cautiously but with unflagging determination. The weak spot in this picture in his or her sensitivity to criticism. Capricorn/Rats lay their lives (and their earthshaking projects) on the line. Other people get jealous and try to chuck them off the mountain. In love the Capricorn/Rat is as steady, but far from romantic. Hold the candles and flowers please and let's just get on with the sex. In bed, there is little or nothing that can rein in this world beater. He or she is a treasure trove of sensual imagination who knows how to take his time."

CAPRICORN/OX - THE STOLID CONSERVATIVE

"The Capricorn born Ox is a down-home conservative thinker. He's persistent and poky, stubborn and resolute. The Capricorn/Ox entertains solely his own highly individualistic opinions on everything, takes little time to consider the "other guy," and can even be accused of a certain spiritual brutality. Capricorn/Oxen are not violent types. But they can be crude—even cruel—in their methods. There won't be many moments of fantasy in this obdurate soul's orderly life. Marriage and family come first. Peccadilloes? Yes. Occasionally. But no casual romp will ever deflect this densely sexual soul from his own bed in his own home where he feels most strongly that he belongs."

CAPRICORN/TIGER - THE RECKLESS CAVALIER

"This whirlwind of staccato remarks and brusque gestures is a living tower of amiable good will. Now you see him, now you don't. And what you see is exactly what you get—congenial speed. The Capricorn born Tiger is easily bored. The concrete density of Capricorn's ambitious nature meets here with the hasty and sympathetic Tiger's bohemian lifestyle. How this person even has so much as a second to stop and pet a puppy or kiss a baby is beyond me. The Capricorn/Tiger is jet-propelled. He has the metabolism of four hummingbirds and the true gift of sincere bonhomie. They can be counted on to marry and raise a family. But they might not often be at home. This energetic person needs to move, build, greet and meet in order to succeed. He or she may fly off almost anywhere at any time to find new kinds of work projects or even to hunt guinea pigs in New Guinea. He is a sexual soul. But is rarely idle enough to fall victim to casual affairs."

CAPRICORN/CAT-RABBIT - THE SUBTLE CAPITALIST

"In this alloy the cautious Cat blends with the prudent Capricorn and creates a person whose ambition is second only to his gift for success. Endowed from the outset with traits that drive him or her toward slow but sure prosperity, the Capricorn/Cat never makes an important decision rapidly, never leaps wildly into any plan or project, never dashes into relationships without running a marketing study on them first. This person possesses natural wisdom. He's dynamic, vigorous and up-to-the-minute modern. But he's also heedful of possible dangers, and can read a threat from miles away. Need I say more? The Capricorn/Cat/Rabbit usually makes money and keeps it. He doesn't want a noisy life crowded with dangers and hangers-on. Peace and quiet wealth are his goals. Love? Yes of course he wants love. But he wants it to be kept discreet and without conflict. He may be slightly hypochondriac, hence is not given to practicing seamy sex or sleeping around. Home is where his heart (and the rest) are most comfortable."

CAPRICORN/DRAGON - THE LORDLY EPICUREAN

"Nobody condemns mediocrity the way the Capricorn/Dragon can. For people born in this combination of signs, prosperity as a result of personal toil amounts to the strongest hedge against the ordinary. The Capricorn/Dragon is special. He or she feels that peculiarity from a young age, realizes its terrible fragility and wants more than anything to be able to hang on to uniqueness forever. Capricorn/Dragon is aware of the pitfalls of upward mobility. He or she knows full well how much of a struggle is required to reach a peaceable victory and call a truce with adversity. But this knowledge does not daunt this angular Dragon subject. Threats and red flags cannot deter the true zealot. There is a nobility about this proud creature. He wants the big house, the upscale car and the united family - if only to keep up appearances. Meanwhile, sexually there is a lot going on behind the scenes. Some of these highly-sexed types have double (even triple) lives. They require a certain amount of thrill and sludge in their sexual activity which is not always available in that noble mansion on the hill. The Capricorn/Dragon is uneasy with duplicity. But he practices it - a lot!"

CAPRICORN/SNAKE - THE MAGNANIMOUS ZEALOT

"An arrogance and aplomb that would frighten Godzilla characterize this match. Capricorn practices what he preaches, puts his ideas to use and is not afraid of his own ambition. Snakes sense things, sniff out solutions and spend a large portion of their lives slinking in and out of crises on the way to the bank, the jeweler's, the airport, their lawyer's office or jail. Snakes often have more flair than brains. But with Capricorn as a mate, who needs brains? What you notice first about this fascinating character is their presence. These are BIG people. Even if they are physically tiny, their bearing and demeanor are not. Impressively arrayed and well surrounded by loyal acolytes, the imperturbable Capricorn/Snake can lead an entire army to victory with a swish of a pony tail. He also has high ideals and is willing to help anyone he deems worthy to get where they need to go in life. Sexual? Oh yes. Do not think for one moment that this cold-blooded, self-assured person is not HOT. They are loaded with sex appeal and they know how to use it. Sex with this irresistible person has an surprisingly tender, romantic side.

CAPRICORN/HORSE - THE CONSCIENTIOUS ENTREPRENEUR

"Count on me!" says the reliable Capricorn/Horse. And believe me, you can. Here is a marriage made in heaven. Capricorn lends solidity and staying power to the somewhat dandified and often insecure Horse character. In his turn, Horse gives this Capricorn manual dexterity and a finely developed sense of his or her own popularity. Always well turned-out and ready to attack new projects, this person rises above the madding crowd with aplomb. There is a crusader here. Here we have a person of high moral standards who is not afraid of hard work and has no time for trifling. His or her sex life could, no doubt, threaten to be a tad dull. But that is hardly the case. Why? Because this person is so attractive, so pervasively present and admirable that lovers will literally stalk him or her to the ends of the earth. When properly approached (with dignity and politesse), The Capricorn born Horse gallops right into the nearest paddock to perform some sexual circus tricks you may not have even imagined."

CAPRICORN/GOAT - THE ROMANTIC GO-GETTER

"The normally lackadaisical Goat personality gets a run for his money when his birthright links him forever to the rigid, dependable, and ambitious Capricorn mountain-climbing Goat. The Chinese Goat and the occidental one are poles apart. The Asian Goat drips with sensitivity and thinks only of whimsy and invention. The other is an uphill skier whose ambition is to be ambitious. "Get there or die!" says the dogged Capricorn. "Ouch! My feet hurt," whines the sensitive Goat. Inner discord is no stranger to people born under the dual sign of Capricorn/Goat. The push-me-pull-you effect that two directly opposite vectors produce in this character causes him or her a lot of personal anguish. Capricorns born in Goat years know they must be serious. They work to get into a position of power. They struggle through studies and often come up the hard way, through the ranks. Both signs are persevering and able. Alongside the rigorous work ethic, this person is a romantic idealist. They make eager and enthusiastic sex partners."

CAPRICORN/MONKEY - THE SCRUPULOUS SOPHISTICATE

"A certain air of resigned melancholy pervades the portrait of Capricorn born in Monkey. Although I cannot say why, the combination of Capricorn-the austere and Monkey, the jaunty problem-solver creates in its natives a queer brand of personal anguish. These people are not obviously nervous. Indeed, their smart demeanor and distinguished bearing bespeak an attitude of self-assurance. Capricorn/Monkeys send out dignity vibes. They are what my mother used to call debonair. Nevertheless, underneath the smooth, mannerly veneer lives a tortured soul. If they are not careful to watch the pattern of their mental health, they might become maniacally clean and neat or obsessively nattily dressed or paranoiacally suspicious. When the anxiety level rises too high, they may also seek solace in drugs or alcohol. The best thing I know about these charmers is that they tell a mean story. Listening to them recount the least chance meeting on a commuter train is always a pleasure. Love for these nervous souls must be true and long lasting. They are choosy about the quality of the person they take to their beds."

CAPRICORN/ROOSTER - THE RETICENT ACHIEVER

"Dignified and impeccable, the Capricorn born Rooster cuts a dashing figure. He will be well turned out, strong of opinion and honest to a fault. Capricorn's reserve matches the conservative side of the Rooster nature harmoniously. There is little conflict and lots of restraint. The Capricorn/Rooster possesses integrity and autonomy. He functions well alone if he has to. But he prefers to be surrounded. Count on the Capricorn/Rooster to do the "done" thing. This person's charm is increased by his excellent manners, his careful use of words, and his ability to find the best in each situation. Capricorn/Roosters worry about how others see them and make heroic efforts to please those who judge their behavior. These people care greatly for appearances but are never guilty of pretension. You won't find one of these noble souls engaged in anything disreputable - even sex! No. This character is faithful to a fault (if such a thing exists) and not attracted to dealing with deep emotion. He or she is easy to love. Everybody does. But intimacy with such a reserved type is a challenge - to say the least."

CAPRICORN/DOG - THE CONCERNED CRITIC

"This is a flinty cobblestone of a person. A mixture of the cozy concrete and the cynical concrete, whose main aim in life is independence and peacekeeping. The Capricorn/Dog is relatively fearful of the abstract, the vague, the metaphysical, and spends a great portion of his life ensuring that what belongs to him stays where it belongs. To clarify, these people are cautious, conservative and conscious of society's demands. They are far from snobs. Instead, they watch and worry while the rest of us debauch and destroy ourselves. The Capricorn/Dog loves order and wishes to preserve it. He almost never restrains himself from blurting out truths - even if they hurt the person they love most. These sweet people are giving and will help out anyone in trouble or danger without thinking twice about consequences. In love (as in all other areas of their lives), Capricorn/Dogs are loyal and true. But they are not crazy about the down and dirty aspects of sex. Sex is messy. Capricorn/Dog people flee mess. To get one of these people into a compromising position is a test of your ability to scratch behind the ears, caress and ultimately to seduce a very touchy watchdog."

CAPRICORN/PIG - THE MERRY MEGALOMANIAC

"This mix creates a being of infinite talent and aspirations to match. The sky is the limit. Capricorn/Pigs never see themselves as less than monstrously famous and hugely wealthy. These folks are grandeur specialists, whose personal goals of cosmic proportions don't stand in the way of their equally epic egos. There is, in the Capricorn/Pig makeup, a certain refreshing purity of desire. No Capricorn/Pig ever underestimates him- or herself. Some claim that such a clearheaded attitude toward blatant self-seeking ambition is healthy. I make no judgment, but I will tell you that most of Capricorn/Pigs I have had the pleasure of knowing have contributed something enriching to my life. This subject undertakes vast artistic projects and gives generously to cultural institutions. The Capricorn/Pig is a faithful and passionate lover. But he is also a smothering one. Possessive is a mild word to describe how they cling to the object of their desire. Scenes. Rows. Rages. Fits. They don't get angry often, but when they do.... run for your life."

AQUARIUS

♒

AQUARIUS/RAT - THE BOHEMIAN BOURGEOIS

"Onward and upward" should be the motto of this completely idealistic, experimental and I might add "majestic" character. Aquarius the individualist married to the aggressive and charming Rat character affords us a being of immense personal magnetism and derring-do. On the one hand, the Aquarian born Rat seeks to accumulate material possessions. On the other, this person cares less about tangibles than I do about Eskimo fertility rites. He's a bohemian with a bourgeois streak. A hippie sophisticate. He wants to be free and unencumbered. But he cannot stand to be alone. He wants to ride a black stallion on the beach in the wind, but he's not mad about horses. A contradictory nature full of excellent intentions, the Aquarius/Rat somersaults through life, stopping only to exhibit the fruits of his immense talent here and there as he tumbles along. Sex with this person is like being on a merry-go- round of pleasure. Mind you, the erotic temperament of Aquarians born in Rat years is very uneven. So you won't be in the amusement park every day of the week. But when you are, it's pure paradise. This creature understands so much about human beings and about life and well...about sex and its peaks and valleys."

AQUARIUS/OX - THE AFFABLE OPPRESSOR

"A strong-minded and loving bully, the Aquarian born in Ox years is destined to a lifetime of slog and struggle uphill against his own unwillingness to conform. Oxen, as you know, always think that the road to happiness is through retirement from the hub of popular activity. Oxen want to be left alone in the country somewhere. Aquarius is more affable, outgoing, flexible, less tundra-like than the Ox. The blend can be a rocky one to live with. This person is a family type who enjoys her work and her children most. Romance, hearts and flowers are not tops on this character's list of priorities. She has a great sense of humor and an admirable lucidity about how complex she really is. I don't recommend this person for passionate love affairs, but they are often excellent cooks - and great storytellers."

AQUARIUS/TIGER - THE ERRATIC TRENDSETTER

"A more speculative Tiger than we already know is personified by this clear-thinking, zigzag personality. Aquarius lends Tiger vision. Tiger congeals some of the free-floating mental jello that characterizes Aquarians. This combination sign provides the world with many innovators. Aquarius/Tigers go crazy for modern methods. They are purveyors of all sorts of new ways of accomplishing old tasks. They are into everything from the dernier cri computer software for pet training to obscure relaxation techniques developed by astronauts in zero gravity. Aquarians are the weirdoes of the zodiac. Tigers are not exactly known for their stability either. So this person can be said to be "marginal" in that he doesn't fancy settling down in a quiet place to raise family or pursue a calm career in dentistry. There is a spirit of revolution here. Aquarian/Tigers want change. Sometimes it's only change for themselves which is why they move about so much. But often they will start a crusade for big change in government or work for feminist or class action causes. Love with this zany character is lots of fun. But it doesn't often last too long. Don't be surprised if you wake up on morning and he or she is long gone - off on another quest for change."

AQUARIUS/CAT-RABBIT - THE ERUDITE EXPLORER

"Here is your true-to-life, one hundred percent virgin intellectual. The Aquarian Cat accumulates knowledge for the fun of it. He is curious about everything, and makes indiscriminate studies of practically everyone he comes in contact with. It doesn't matter whether the subject is edifying or not, Aquarius/Cat wants to know all about it in goriest detail. He's fascinated by knowledge, facts, information, learning, erudition—and experience. He or she spends a lifetime leaping from book to book, from museum to museum, and from discipline to other discipline. It's Cats born in Aquarius like to do—know more. These folks have a varied love life. Always seeking the exotic and different, they often end up married to a person from another culture who speaks ten languages and can teach them all. One thing is sure, if you take up with one of these characters, you will never be bored."

AQUARIUS/DRAGON - THE FUN-LOVING CONQUEROR

"I know" and "I preside" were walking across the bridge. One of them fell in. Who was left? That's correct! No matter which way you look at this character, he's right up there in the top twenty. You see, Aquarius/Dragon always takes over. Nothing can stop him, as he both knows and presides better than everybody else. There is a driving, steady quality to this personality. No matter what he or she does it will be accomplished with flourish and style. Aquarius born Dragons are brainy, yet circumspect about showing it. They are family-oriented and respect social conventions. Yet, they never want to miss out on a fascinating career. So they charge ahead, winning contests and receiving praise and prizes every step of the way. Marriage? Love? Sex? Yes but... Career first. Conquering the world is somehow more important to this powerful creature than wasting time nuzzling somebody's neck during a cocktail party."

AQUARIUS/SNAKE - THE DOTING INTUITIVE

"Sunshine incarnate, the Snake born in Aquarius has the double luck to be able to think clearly and to intuit things with rare finesse. This "up" person is firmly planted in reality, yet manages to keep smiling. He is a natural optimist and stubborn about maintaining that image. The Aquarius/Snake never bothers to want what he knows he cannot have. Nonetheless, he is avid for what he desires and can get. By this I mean that the Serpent born in Aquarius is chillingly lucid. He or she will attempt to seduce and conquer others for the sheer excitement of the dance. But before attempting to seduce or entice, enchant or charm, this person will know well ahead precisely what his chances are. Snakes born in Aquarius do not play losing games. Love is all important to this character. He or she will need plenty of sex - even the experimental kinds. A caring and willing bed partner, this loving creature is passionate, but never loses his head. If ever you fall in love with one of these sexually adventurous types, you will see what the words "sexually imaginative" really mean."

AQUARIUS/HORSE - THE GALLOPING VISIONARY

"To this alert and energetic Aquarian, variety and movement represent freedom. The Horse lends rebellion to the clear-minded Aquarian, and pushes him to stride ahead. Horses are hasty and gifted for easy accomplishment. The Aquarian wants an original life. When the two are matched by birth, an eccentric, fleeting sort of being evolves. The Aquarius/Horse never lights for long. Sex, is of course, a must for this galloping visionary. However as he doesn't fancy settling down to raise up a herd of ponies, he will be more the type of lover who flits from flower to flower, loving and leaving onward and upward. This is not to say that the Aquarius born Horse is not a great lover. He or she will be an ardent and exciting partner in bed. But not for long. Something new and unusual will catch his eye and off he goes into the sunset."

AQUARIUS/GOAT - THE INVENTIVE FUTURIST

Aquarius weds the Goat. Clarity and sensitivity, knowledge and whimsy. This solid marriage of complementary signs is rich with possibilities. Aquarius brings a dowry of independence to the inconsistent Goat, whose byword is dependency. Goat carries emotional depth with him to the wedding. This Aquarius can feel more profoundly than most. And his Goat identity benefits from an electrical charge of true Aquarian autonomy. This person will be gifted for futuristic planning, oblivious to social criticism, and capable of maddening individuality. Invention belongs to this person. He or she can imagine novel solutions to common problems and work through weeks night and day getting the concept on its feet. And Love? The poor Aquarius/Goat never seems to get enough of it. He gobbles sex. He is known to be fickle and further not to understand why his mate is jealous. He's not jealous. He's openhearted and free thinking. Marriage for this person is "iffy" at best."

AQUARIUS/MONKEY - THE MAJOR PLAYER

"A person of exceptional breadth and depth arises from the union of Aquarius and Monkey. The natural detachment of Aquarius assists the Monkey in forging his destiny without cumbersome sentiment or extraneous emotion. Monkey gives the visionary Aquarian a sound sense of fact and helps him to deal with the present. The combination is harmonious and promising. It produces real heavyweights in the brains department. Great deeds can be accomplished by this serious (somewhat revolutionary) person. Aquarius/Monkeys are gifted with exceptional scope in their way of looking at the world. This giant of a person doesn't often look to passion as a panacea. He or she will love and probably even marry. But they would never sacrifice their mission for a mad love affair."

AQUARIUS/ROOSTER - THE FLEXIBLE FLYER

"First of all, the Aquarius born in a Rooster year often succeeds. And second of all, he frequently fails. The Rooster's swings of good and bad luck go on through the whole of his life, no matter what astrological sign he was born under. However (and here's the big however), Aquarius, the offbeat and aloof sign of brotherly love and general good will, possesses just the quality Roosters have been waiting for to keep them from scratching around in the dust for an errant grain of corn for years until their luck returns. Aquarians are lucid visionaries whose very detachment, although at times maddening, saves the Rooster. This person is an original. Nobody really ever understands him or her or comprehends their outlandish notions. They are loving and true in marriage and family matters. But they are mostly interested in how to beat the system which they always find gets in the way of their personal progress. Sexually, these characters will surprise you by their tender gestures and erotic..."

AQUARIUS/DOG - THE BRASH RESCUER

"The Aquarius is a Dog of the Saint Bernard persuasion. He caretakes. She lends a hand, holds a weary head and comforts those less lucky than herself. In the process of all this philanthropic service and apparently selfless loving, the Aquarius/Dog takes great pains to look after himself as well. He can be bossy and power-hungry and, what's more, the Aquarius/Dog makes no bones about masking his ambitions in charity's raiment. He may be making a million dollars a year, but since he's doing it for a cause or teaching somebody something, or bringing them pleasure, why shouldn't he live in abject luxury? His love life is a patchwork of complication. She may take up with a married man, urge him to divorce so he can be free to love only her and then announce that she herself is married. The Aquarius/Dog is a complex person for whom love and sex are not necessarily intertwined. His sexual escapades are many and often tinged with the exotic."

AQUARIUS/PIG - THE AUDACIOUS ARTIST

"There evolves from the blend of Aquarius with Pig a brash quality that borders on lumpishness. Perhaps the Pig's naturally pastoral, countrified side imitates Aquarius's openness. Or maybe the Aquarian subject picks excess sincerity from the Pig and becomes too direct. But whatever the mechanics, this subject comes up both bold and forward. These people are aggressively charismatic. They know how to attract crowds and please them. Love is of the utmost importance to this reckless creature. His whisperings are full of sensuous innuendo and promises of marvelous sexual surprise. But when the lights are low and he or she gets you into bed, you might be surprised at how UN surprised you are by the follow up."

PISCES

♓

PISCES/RAT - THE INSIDE OUTSIDER

"This incisive character, a wizard by combination of receptivity and offense, serves best as half of a team. If there is one person who can play the game in hand with a partner and win almost every time, due to the very energy created by the partnership, it's the Pisces/Rat. Neither Pisces nor Rat characters are natural hermits. The Pisces, extra sensitive and watery, when allied to the power-hungry Rat gains a certain perspective on the finite that assures him an exceptional ability to make wise choices. Their greatest strength is adaptability. Love? Well, it's a bit complicated for the Pisces/Rat because he is nervous and high strung. He requires a mate or significant other who can shoulder and comfort him when the chips are down. As a sexual partner, this person is affectionate and tender. The really passionate parts are not printable here."

PISCES/OX - THE WISE DREAMER

"The Pisces born in an Ox year is quite a character. Just when you think this person is nothing more than froth and furbelow, thwack! He or she floors you with a remark that would knock the wind out of Chicago. The gap between the basic slugger nature of Oxen and Pisces' ephemeralness misleads one. Never forget that you can't judge a book by its cover. The Pisces/Ox seems for all the world the artiste, the stereotypical Pisces dreamer. But wait! Pisces/Ox is perhaps even more of a schemer than a poet. There is a huge capacity for work and follow through with this savvy character. He or she will also be loyal in friendship and able to conform to social convention. Love? Yes. These folks are gifted for marriage and enjoy being settled with one person for life. Sex? The Pisces/Ox may stray from time to time. But he or she doesn't take such peccadilloes seriously and always remains discreet."

PISCES/TIGER – THE BLITHEST SPIRIT

"This plucky Pisces character spends a large chunk of his energy and time trying to achieve closer rapport with himself. Pisces born in Tiger years often feel confined by their spunky feline side and sometimes wish to shake the Tiger off their backs. Pisces likes to swim in limitless time and move through infinite space. Constraints are of no interest to the Fish. He longs to be free to float unbound. His goal is spiritual enlightenment and personal equilibrium. He is moreover, a very hard worker. Luck is with this Tiger because of his ability to adapt to whatever circumstance is available to him. Besides, people like him instantly. He's open and up front about what he wants and is not afraid to go after it. AND... He or she is crack-me-up funny. In love he may be a tad flighty while still young. But after thirty, he or she usually settles down and can be monogamous. A delicious sex partner is this character. He's caring and tender and he is moreover a laugh riot."

PISCES/CAT-RABBIT – THE SOPHISTICATED INDEPENDENT

"Does the Cat dip his paw in the water and eat up the unsuspecting Fish? No. This lovely couple has a happy beginning and equally felicitous ending. Pisces' sensitivity blends swimmingly well with the Cat's love of hearth and home, caution and modesty. The Piscean born in a Cat year will probably enjoy a long and productive career as a guardian of refinement and elegance. He or she is almost assured of having artistic talents and, moreover, can count on knowing how to put those same talents to practical and profitable use. There's a need for social acceptance here too. This character wants whatever he or she does to imprint itself on society. In love, he or she will not be flashy or showy. They often marry quietly somewhere and live away from crowds. He needs tenderness and affection and gives lots in return."

PISCES/DRAGON THE MERRY MOVER

"The Fish born in Dragon cares greatly for his or her own advancement. This person needs to feel progress. Standing still renders him nervous and edgy. So, when there is no progress, if he is not moving ahead, he travels. One thing is sure; the Pisces born Dragon is a mover. He may be running or walking, swimming or taking a train, but the Fish/Dragon ambulates. The Pisces/Dragon is always fun to be around. He or she has always got a quip for you or a party to invite you to. In love this character is not terribly constant. He's almost too attractive to the opposite sex and requires tons of different experiences to keep his ego shiny and bright. The best thing about this fickle creature is that when an affair is over, he doesn't hold a grudge. He's sentimental and forgiving. He goes on loving even when love has flown up the chimney."

PISCES/SNAKE - THE PROVOCATIVE ORACLE

"This deep thinker is bubbly and graceful but only on the strict surface. Underneath roil philosophies and perceptions too otherworldly to share with any but the most enlightened. Pisces/Snake feels everything profoundly and intuits each situation with such force and lucidity that he almost winces at the power of human contact. Sensitivity takes on a whole new meaning in the case of the Pisces/Snake. Intuition is redoubled, second sight emphasized and presentiment so powerful as to be considered a gift. Pisces/Snake is a kind of witch in sheep's clothing. And is he or she attractive? This person actually magnetizes the opposite sex. People can't keep their hands of this gorgeous creature. True love, for the Pisces/Snake has no bounds. He or she will most likely find a mate early on and settle down directly. As he is more a philosopher and thinker than a sexpot, the mate he or she chooses may eventually stray."

PISCES/HORSE - THE BEGUILING ARTISTE

"The apparent peacefulness of this combination of Fish and Horse is but a fine shell surrounding a highly fragile and spiritual nature. Pisces/Horse people are both clairvoyant and humanistic. They give of themselves without expecting more than a pat on the head in return. In this double sign, the Horse's ordinarily selfish push for autonomy is quieted. Pisces keeps the Horse's dander down, teaches him to be self-effacing, and shows him the wonders of clairvoyance. The Pisces/Horse is well-advised to find a real passion (music, dance, art, building or even business) while still young and follow his or her star throughout his entire life. If he waits too long to find his path, he may become distracted and fritter away his energies looking for just the right profession. In love the Pisces born Horse has the capacity for undying devotion. He or she may be slightly on the shy side in bed. But the intuitive mate will know how to turn this charming creature on with tons of reassurance and smooches. In turn, he will admire and applaud his mate for bringing him pleasure."

PISCES/GOAT - THE SUCCESSFUL CREATIVE

"This person, a combination of the two most sensitive, feeling signs of both zodiacs, is what the French call "un grand sensible." This character's sensitivity comes first. The rest—the genius, the ability to apply talents, the romance and the soul—come later. I always used to imagine that a person born under this ensemble of signs might prove so hypersentient as to be perfectly useless in the real world. But now I realize, after collecting a bunch of these people and watching them live, that my image of the writhing poet in pain from the very sound of his own inspiration

is totally false. Pisces born in Goat are some of the most powerful Pisces. Great deeds of an artistic and even political nature are possible here. The Pisces born Goat is wise. He is at one with himself and does not suffer from inner conflicts. As a result, his brains and sensitivities work together to help make him a world class crackerjack at whatever her chooses to do. Love? Well, real intimacy is difficult for this very psychic, gifted person. He doesn't have much time for noodling around at the mall looking for shoes for the baby or selecting a perfume for his wife. The Pisces/Goat is "other" and so, if he or she marries, must seek a partner who can run his or her world while he gets on with the business of being a genius. Sex? Of course he has sex. But you would never know it."

PISCES/MONKEY - THE CUNNING ACCOMPLICE

"The merry monkey finds a new, more elegant external image under the influence of unrestrained Pisces. The Monkey is normally levelheaded. His job in the Chinese Zodiac is to solve problems, big and small. Monkeys are born with common sense. Monkeys are natural leaders but not power seekers. They have cunning and stability. A rare combination. Pisces lends spiritual grace and beauty to the nimble and spirited Monkey. The result is a handsome person whose reputation for charm precedes him or her everywhere. This person is also very kind and charitable and giving. Their love life? Madness. Passion. Drama. Thing is, this character is too damned good-looking and dashing not to be pursued by fanatical fans everywhere he or she goes. Result? Long, stormy love affairs and epic marriages of the angry plate throwing variety. Having such a beautiful, appealing mate is bound to cause his partner pain and create jealousies. How does this person make love? Often."

PISCES/ROOSTER - THE CLOSET INTELLECTUAL

"The greatest quality of the combination of Fish and Rooster is resiliency and the ability to adapt to any given environment. This thorough and self-directed person feels instantly at home wherever he or she happens to be sitting. They like change, and move quickly to adjust and acclimatize. Roosters are adventurous. Pisces like to wander. Moving through space attracts this enthusiastic character. Discord causes the Pisces/Rooster to flee. Unrequited love makes him weep. This person is often in (and out) of love. The reason for this (to my mind anyway) is that he deems himself perfect. He doesn't see that he has faults. All communication stops when this person refuses to acknowledge his own errors and love commits suicide right before his eyes. The Pisces born Rooster then feels sorry for him/herself. Nobody understands. Boo hoo. If you love such a creature, refuse to put up with his self pity. And take him to a therapist who can make him admit when he's wrong."

PISCES/DOG - THE SARCASTIC SOFTIE

"The Pisces born in a Dog year, like all Pisceans only more so, has a tender side that must be nurtured and treated with sincere affection.. Their sensitivity takes the form of nervous touchiness. They don't like to be questioned or contradicted. They are strong-minded but can be weak-willed. There is a charming, childlike quality to these attractive people and one wants to protect them. The Pisces/Dog is usually married. They thrive on security in matters of the heart and don't even mind being bossed around a bit by someone they see as stronger and more capable than they. This person loves the way we all dream of being loved: tenderly and with real deep feeling and romance. If you have to luck to find yourself entwined with a Pisces born in a Dog year, don't disentangle yourself. Stay right where you are and enjoy the ride."

PISCES/PIG - THE SENTIENT CLASSICIST

"The degree of permeability in the Pisces/Pig subject is so elevated as to cause him or her a real burden. This person feels more deeply than we do. Pisces/Pigs are gentle souls with unlimited ambition. They are sensualists who love luxe and care immensely for tradition and custom. I'd say without hesitation that the Pisces/Pig's biggest stumbling block is the modern world. He is old-fashioned and firmly rooted in time-honored ways. Shortcuts irritate the Pisces/Pig. Nicknames grate on his nerves. Gadgets bore him. Some people accuse this person of being a clinging vine in matters of the heart. It's fully understandable because the Pisces born Pig needs the security of full-time affection and tenderness in order to survive. Without fervent full time love, he feels shipwrecked and alone. He will go to great lengths to hang onto an object of desire. Nothing, for the Pisces/Pig, can replace true love. His sex drive is known for being a tad over the top."

http://suzannewhite.com/astrology/newAstrology.html

ABOUT THE AUTHOR

Best Selling author Suzanne White is American. She often lives in France and Buenos Aires. Suzanne speaks French, English and Spanish. She has been a college professor, a fashion model, a journalist, an interpreter, a novelist, a fireworks salesperson, director of a Parisian Couture boutique, an elevator operator, a shoe salesperson, a single mother and a simultaneous translator. She came to writing late at age 33. By age 38, she had written her first best seller. THE NEW ASTROLOGY™, A savvy fusion of Chinese and Western astrological signs creating 144 NEW SIGNS. Suzanne White's fans and readers have dubbed her: "The High Priestess" of Chinese and Western Astrologies. Suzanne's books are on every best seller list worldwide. She does Private Chart Readings and answers all e-mail personally. suzanwhite@aol.com

###

Printed in Great Britain
by Amazon

35312010R00031